Why Consistency
and How to Be Consistent
to Achieve Any Goal

Charles I. Prosper

First Edition • November 2015

Global Publishing Company • Los Angeles, California

Other Books By Charles I. Prosper

The 12 Secrets of Success

207 Inspirational Quotes of Charles I. Prosper

How to Get Fit Fast at Any Age

Books By Luzemily Prosper

The Sayings of Luzemily, The 7-Year Old Sage

To my friend Joseph Daniel, one of the wisest and most consistenly brilliant persons that I know

Why Consistency is the Key to All Success – and How to Be Consistent to Achieve Any Goal

Charles I. Prosper

Book layout design and cover design by Charles I. Prosper

LIBRARY OF CONGRESS CATALOG CARD DATA

ISBN–13 978-0-943845-80-7

PRINTED IN THE UNITED STATES OF AMERICA

12 11 10 9 8 7 6 5 4 3 2 1

Contents

"It's not what you know, but what you consistently do with what you know that makes a difference." – *Charles I. Prosper*

INTRODUCTION

I first became interested in this subject of consistency when I decided to get back into excellent physical shape by enrolling in my neighborhood *24-Hour Fitness* gym and commit myself to regular daily exercise. The problem, or shall I say the challenge of this was that the only way that I could do this in a consistent and practical way was to get up and do my weight-training exercise routine in the morning before I started my work day.

The only footnote of this plan is that I would have to get up at 4:20 a.m. in order to eat, meditate, dress for the gym, exercise, and be back home by 6:15 a.m. in order to get my 16-year-old daughter, Luzemily (single-dad duties) her breakfast prepared, and get myself ready to drop her off to school before going to work for 8:30 a.m.

To get into the routine of getting up at 4:20 a.m. and becoming and remaining consistent was not an overnight process. (I have been successfully carrying out this commitment, at this moment, for over six months.) It has not been easy, and there are still some days that I struggle to get up and "just do it."

My next challenge to understanding and grasping the meaning of consistency and commitment, which are two sides of the same coin, was in trying to decide, now that I had gotten into the routine, albeit difficult, of getting up at 4:20 a.m. to excercise before starting my work day, is when would I have, or rather make, the time to consistently write 1 hour per day on this book, ironically, on the subject of *consistency*, the book that you are holding in your hands right now.

After dancing around with the idea of what time would be the most practical hour to write this book, I concluded, with a gulp in my throat, that 3:30 a.m. would have to be the time to make my writing schedule possible.

Now don't get me wrong, I am no super-human being endowed with powers of commitment and discipline far beyond those of mortal men. I am just like you. There was no way on Earth that I wanted to get up at 3:30 a.m. to write a book on consistency. I like my sleep and the warm covers of my bed just like any normal human being. And there was no way that I was going to get up yet another hour *earlier* than 4:20 a.m. to write a book. *Hah!* Famous last words!

Well, here I am at 3:30 a.m., after much resistance and much kicking and screaming as I finally dragged myself to the keyboard and have begun to write this book for you. How I managed to do both of these tasks and do them on a consistent basis is the subject of this book.

Writing this book has become the study and the practice of goal-achievement through consistency. What I have learned about consistency is that it does not come by default of having begun anything that you have deemed worthwhile. This is to say that consistency is contrary to human nature. Consistency requires effort. Consistency requires discipline. Consistency requires commitment. And consistency requires that you not only go beyond your comfort zone, but that you do it day-after-day, week-after-week, in a repeated non-stop routine of on-going determination. Consistency is definitely not for the weak or faint of heart. Average people are not consistent; only successful people are consistent. This is the reason why "average" people are in the *majority*, and above-average people, that is, those people who achieve their goals of health, happiness, and prosperity are in the *minority*.

In spite of the ostensibly unattractive nature of consistency, consistency is the angel that will lead you to the fulfillment of all of your goals, dreams, and deepest held life purposes.

In short, consistency is the key to all success, not some success - but all success. No matter how brilliant the plan, no matter how exciting the idea, no matter how "fool-proof" the formula, nothing will result, in the final analysis, unless the plan, the idea, or the "fool-proof" formula is carried out consistently.

Consistency is a statement of faith, in yourself, and in the nature of how the Universe works. If you step back a bit and look at the macrocosm of Life, we see that everything moves and beats in consistent and rhytmical cycles. Life is movement, a consistent non-stop movement. The secret of success has always been staring us in the face, all around us in nature, whenever and wherever we turn.

In this book, I will show you the principles of how to take yourself from where you are to where you want to be. Consistency is the key. Consistency is the only doorway to success. Consistency is what will get you there, and consistency is what will *keep* you there. You will learn that consistency is inevitable. You can't get around it. You are either consistently progressing by choice, or you are consistently retrogressing by default. Nothing stands still; this is the law of life–the law of growth or decay.

Consistency is the key to all success, and you can learn to be consistent to achieve any goal.

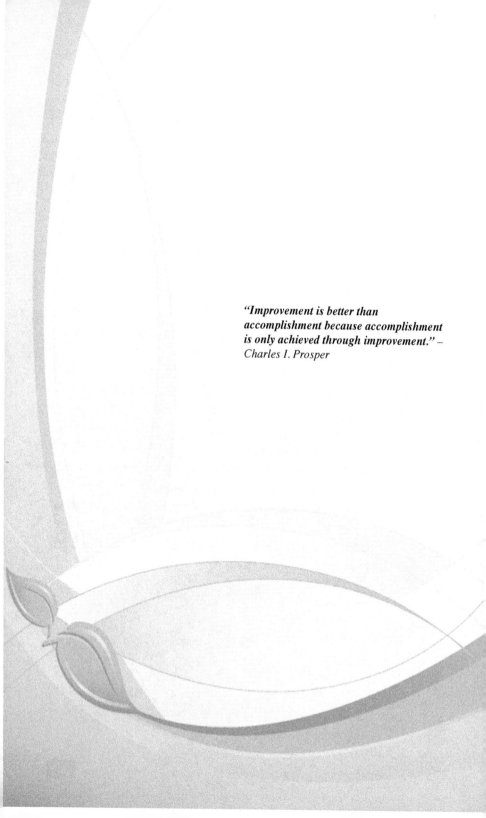

"Improvement is better than accomplishment because accomplishment is only achieved through improvement." –
Charles I. Prosper

What Is Consistency?

So before we begin our journey to the understanding and mastery of consistency, it would be appropriate to ask, "What is consistency?" Consistency, in my opinion, is both mystical and magical because the impetus behind consistency and the thread which runs through it is faith, vision, and willingness. The Universe rewards action. More importantly, the Universe rewards *consistent* action. The rewards of consistency are many, and eventually they take on the form of euphoria, achievement, enjoyment of life, and the feeling of a sense of purpose.

Consistency *starts* with an idea or inspiration to achieve or to do something that usually require time, discipline, and a constant effort on a repeated daily basis. Keep in mind that consistency is not: the time, discipline, and constant effort; time, discipline, and constant effort are the *elements* which propel and move the consistency forward.

After the idea has germinated and set itself within you, a plan of action is the path to realizing where your idea must go. Your plan is the path which must be traveled in order to move from the point where you are now to the point where you wish to be. The plan is your vehicle. Persistence fuels the motor of your vehicle, and consistency is the "straight" line from point A to point B. Point A is your starting point; point

B is your ultimate destination.

There is a certain sameness or routine that is at the core of consistency. *Webster's New World Dictionary*, 2003, page 142, defines **con-sis´ten-cy** as "conformity with previous practice." So, for consitency to work, it must conform with some previous practice that has been designed as part of a well-thought out plan.

In order to be successful with my weight-training exercise routine, I must design and plan a series of exercises that must be repeated in an intelligent pattern of progressive resistance. In order for the eating and diet part of my health regime to work, in harmony with my weight-training, I must eat in a certain way everyday, that has scientifically been proven to produce the specific results that I seek.

In order for anyone to know or trust me, I must behave in a consistently reliable and trustworthy manner. Consistency is what keeps the Universe together and the planets from colliding as they intelligently revolve in a repeated rhythmical and reliable pattern. (More on this later.)

When Do Yo Know Consistency Has Started?

We have a goal. We have a plan. We have made a decision to begin. We take action and begin according to plan. At what point can we say that consistency has begun? I believe that it can be said that consistency has begun the moment you have successfully repeated the pattern of your plan a second time and a third time without skipping according to your scheduled activity.

Consistency is a non-stop continuum as we move closer and closer to a chosen goal. Part of the goal of consistency is to be as consistent as possible. The goal is to become 100% consistent with carrying out the action-plan of our commitment. This leads us now to a practical consideration and question.

Is Perfect Consistency Always Possible?

Yes and no. Perfect consistency is possible in theory, but not 100% probable in practice. Life is full of inconsistent events that can and will occasionally impact and impede our practice of consistent performance.

You have been getting up to go to the gym everyday now for the last 3 weeks, and you are feeling great about yourself. Your daughter wakes up with a fever, and you have to take her to the doctor for an early emergency appointment. You will have to skip your morning workout for this day. You have been writing 5 pages of your book everyday for over a month from 5:30 to 8:00 p.m. You get a call from your childhood best-friend who has just arrived at the airport and needs for you to pick him up. Your writing schedule has just been interrupted for now.

The danger in giving these situational explanations is that those who are looking for an excuse to skip or to not to continue will certainly find one. Saying that perfect consistency is not always 100% is not an argument for complacency or a plea for mediocrity; the goal is *always* to aim for 100% consistency. However, 97 to 99% consistency is not only possible but practical and probable, and will eventually take us to our goal.

Are Consistency and Persistence the Same?

Is there a difference between consistency and persistence? And if there is a difference, what part does persistence play in the achievement of your goal?

There is indeed a difference between consistency and persistence because the success of your objective is predicated on how persistent you are when unexpected events get in the way of the performance of your plan. *Webster's New World Dictionary*, 2003, page 481, defines **per-sist´tent** as "continuing, esp. in the face of opposition, etc."

Consistency is a Theoretical Straight Line

In order to understand the part that persistence plays in the achievement of consistency, we might consider the theoretical construct of consistency as a metaphorical straight line.

Consistency is a straight path, which leads to your goal. In a perfect world, with "all things being equal," once you have decided and have begun to move toward your goal, as long as you continue to move forward, you will inevitably get there without question. However, we do not live in a perfect world, and all things are *never* equal, for the nature of life itself is that change and unpredictability always happen.

Our goals and decisions are subject to be impacted by a myriad of unexpected and unpredicatable events, which may attempt to throw us off course in the pursuit of our dream. (If goal-achievement were that easy, then everybody would be doing it.) Goal-achievement is beset with many challenges and distractions along the path.

Another consideration is that mathematical science has never been able to prove the existence of a perfectly straight line in any geometrical example. They have come close, but a perfectly straight line has never been created, and in my opinion, can never exist. A perfectly straight line, just like a "perfect vacuum" are both a type of "scientific fantasy," theoretically created by some visionary PhD, who'd like to give him or herself the illusion of control.

We may still *consider* consistency a straight-line-path to our objective, however, we know that challenges, the unexpected and unpredictable events can impact our forward movement and occasionally throw us off course. This is where persistence comes in. We start off moving forward in a straight line, and some challenge or unexpected event temporarily throws us off course, persistence is that which puts us quickly *back* on course. The stronger the persistence, the *faster* we get back on course and the longer will tend to stay on course.

An airplane that takes off has a charted course to arrive at a given destination, which could be plotted as a straight line. However, anyone who has even flown in a airplane frequently enough has learned that external factors, such as airpockets, or tempestuous weather, will cause the plane to temporarily move off course, however, the internal computer-controlled guidance systems will quickly move the plane back on course as soon as it is possible.

The airplane's computer-controlled guidance system can be likened to our persistence, which always puts us back on track if we are unexpectedly thrown off course.

So, because of persistence, and in spite of external or internal distractions, we move back on course toward our goal as soon as possible, and as such, move *not* in a perfectly straight line but in more of a zig-zag pattern of "getting slightly off course then back on course," slightly off course, then back on course, until we eventually reach our destination.

The stronger the persistence, the less likely we will be thrown off course. The stronger the persistence, the faster we get back on track. The stronger the persistence, the longer we are likely to *stay* on track before another challenge can possibly throw us off track.

The strength of persistence is predicated on the willingness to renew our determination and commitment on a daily basis. We choose to commit and persist this day, but this commitment and persistence has to be renewed the next day, and the next, and the next. You cannot be persistent for that which *may* happen tomorrow. You are only responsible for your persistence of *this* day. Every day counts. Each day that your task is successfully completed, another step has moved you closer to where you want to be. Consistency is a task-by-task, day-by-day proposition. The cycle (circle) of success is: willingness to act, followed by immediate action, followed by persistence, and followed by the willingness to act again. The wheel turns each day, thus moving you closer and closer to your goal.

Connected Consistency

Connected consistency is when one action depends upon another in order to be consistent. Allow me to explain. I am writing this book on consistency, and it is currently 3:52 a.m. I may make it sound easy, but it isn't. I find it to be a monumental task at times, when I would much rather just stay in bed and sleep like "normal" people.

In order for me to be consistent in order to get up every morning at 3:30 a.m., I *have* to go to bed no later than 8:30 p.m. Ideally, my head should hit the pillow by 8:00 p.m. If I am not consistent with this time I that go to bed, I will not be consistent with the time I must wake up.

Another example. At 5:30 a.m., I go to the gym to lift weights and exercise. If I do not consistently prepare myself an adequate breakfast of, say, oatmeal, egg whites, and a piece of fresh fruit, I will not be able to workout with the energy and intensity that is required to get the results that I seek. The consistency of my workouts is predicated on my eating and sleeping habits. This is what I mean by connected consistency.

Let us say that you consistently want to save $500.00 per month for over two years for the purpose of saving the down payment on your first home or property. The connected consistency, in this case, could be the need to start another savings account in which you would place $100 per month. This second savings account would be your "go-to" emergency reserves which would sit in front of your real estate savings account, thus keeping you from dipping into and taking out any money during your two-year commitment.

If we look closely at almost any important endeavor, with the end result of important goal-achievement, there is usually so sort of connected consistency that prepares the way for the success of the goals we seek.

Patience Is a Magic Component of Consistency

Consistency would not be difficult or very challenging if consistency was just a matter of doing something successfully once, and all of life's health, happiness, success, prosperity, and peace of mind would be ours. Tacitly, the underlying challenge inherent in almost all consistent endeavors of an important goal is that it usually will happen over time, and because of the time factor, patience becomes inevitable.

Almost anyone can be consistent on the short term, but the real magic begins when consistency is carried through repeatedly and successfully on the *long* term.

Here's the key. Patience requires faith, and faith requires courage. Courage comes from within, and I believe that courage can only come from within until one is willing and open to be guided by some Power or Intelligence that is greater than him or herself.

Let's take a practical example. As of this month, I have decided and committed to saving $2000 per month for the next 2 years. Patience and courage become a key component to the success of this goal. Consistency is due to be challenged by the vicissitudes of internal and external temptations and doubt. Have you ever tried to save certain amount of money and before you get there, you are tempted by the thought "I need to do, such-and-such, so, I can just borrow a few hundred dollars from myself and replace it next month"?

The problem with this is that you can never "replace" any saved money that you "borrow" from yourself because the money that you put back into your account the next month – *is not the same money!* The money you took out is gone; you are starting all over again.

Patience requires courage, and courage requires the willingness to "suffer" or at least to be uncomfortable long enough in order to face and withstand the "intruder thoughts" whose only purpose is to distract you from whom you have decided to be.

Consistency Requires a Plan within Which to Operate

Let us review our basics. *Webster's New World Dictionary,* 2003, page 142, defines **con-sis´ten-cy** as "conformity with previous practice." Consistency requires a plan, and a plan is no more than an agreement with yourself to do a certain thing in a certain way in some structure or organized way. One of the words which describes the *Webster* definition of consistency is the word "conformity." *Webster's New World Dictionary,* 2003, page 140, defines **con-form** as "to be in agreement."

Consistency is the plan or path that points to and leads us to our objective. In considering the probable success of our strides forward, it could be said that the more careful and well thought-out the plan, the more likely one will remain on course and thereby remain consistent.

If I say that I will get up every morning and do 200 situps for the next 6 months, even though I have not done any serious exercise for a few years is not likely to lead to my consistent performance of this plan. However, considering the particulars of this example, were I to start with 10 situps a day, and then, every week, increase the situps by 5, as I became stronger and more physically fit, the likelihood of my gradually reaching the 200-situp-per-day mark within this 6-month-period become very probable and highly likely.

Consistency Starts with a Goal

All throughout these beginning pages, I have alluded to the fact that a goal or an objective is necessary first in order for the idea of consistency to become relevant. We have to have *something* for which to become consistent. Consistent for *what?* – is the question.

Once a goal has been chosen, the next step is the creation of an intelligent plan that is likely to lead us there with the least amount of distractions. What moves us forward, however, is motivation and desire, and what creates motivation is *value.*

Value Determines Motivation

I think that it is a fair question to ask, what determines motivation? What is it that keeps us consistent? Why is it that some will continue while others (i.e. most) will start and usually quit?

The answer to both of these questions lies in the extent to which an individual understands and keeps in mind the importance or seriousness of the objective that is set before him. In a word, once we see and understand the value of that which we seek, the concomitant determination, desire, and motivation become inevitable.

Ask the "average" working man or woman to save an extra $500 a month for the next two months, assuming that he or she has never been in the habit of saving money, is not likely to get an enthusiastic response. He or she is likely to say, "I can't afford to save that much money this month; I have so many bills to pay that I hardly have anything left over." Little perceived value of the idea of savings leads to little or no motivation to take action and make it happen.

Same man or woman but a slightly different situation. This person has just got the unfortunate and shocking news that their 7-year-old daughter is in need of an operation to remove an inflamed appendix, and that they will have to raise $1000 in the next 60 days to save her life. Do you think in your wildest dreams that this parent would have *any* problem in saving and raising this money now? I think that the answer is obvious. When I propose this question and imaginary situation to people, the answer is always a resounding, "Of course I would save that money up! To save my child, it would be a piece of cake!"

However, I believe that the question of the motivation for consistency is not necessarily the need to have a life or death crisis in order for us to move with alacrity, it is a question of the need to have the wisdom of understanding the value of what we have chosen to accomplish and to remind ourselves of the value of our objective on a regular and daily basis.

Consistency Is Predicated on a Schedule

If I have learned anything about consistency it is that consistency requires a schedule. The very definition of consistency implies that a schedule must exist in order for consistency to exist. Consistency is defined as "conformity with previous practice;" *Webster's New World Dictionary,* 2003, page 574, defines **scedule** as "a timed plan for a project."

I am reminded of the importance of schedule in order to remain consistent everytime I deviate from my routine. For the last several weeks, I have successfully been able to go to bed at 8:30 p.m., and I have successfully gotten up at 3:30 a.m. in order to write this book.

Last night was Friday, so I didn't have to worry about getting up super-early to go to work on Saturday, my day off. So, I watched the animated 1999 Disney movie, *Tarzan,* with Luzemily until about 11:10 p.m. I got to sleep about 11:30 p.m., and I woke up at 8:00 a.m. Even though I got roughly a little more sleep than I normally would during the week, my *rhythm* for writing was thrown off so much that I literally had to *force* myself to start, which took me almost an hour to begin. Normally, had I woken up at 3:30 a.m., I would have begun writing within fives minutes of having gotten up.

The key to consistency is rhythm. Same-time, same-place is the secret. Consistency is a cycle. Consistency is a heartbeat. Consistency is an inhalation and exhalation. Consistency is winter, spring, summer, and fall. Consistency is dawn, day, dusk, and night. Consistency is going to bed at 8:30 p.m. and waking up at 3:30 a.m. Consistency is writing every morning instead of writing: sometimes in the morning, sometimes in the afternoon, or sometimes just before going to bed. The Universe rewards rhythm. The Universe *is* rhythm itself.

Consistency Requires Regularity

That consistency requires regularity is another way of saying that there must be a scheduled plan that is to be executed in an organized and timely manner. Any organized practice regularly done, gathers momentum and power with each repetition. What starts out as a difficult routine in the beginning becomes easy in time and with continued practice.

Discipline is only discipline in the beginning stages; what I mean to say is that discipline is only *difficult* in the beginning stages. Each time that you direct yourself to do what you must do, discipline gradually dissipates and eventually disappears thus transmuting the activity into the joy of being and doing, which can become part of a new way of life for you.

Regularity requires loyalty. Should you stop your regular practice, you begin to revert back to your original state. This can be seen quite clearly in the area of physical fitness. You may resist with all of your being the idea of going to a gym and working out on a regular schedule of same-time, same-place everyday. If you are like most people, to begin such a schedule means "discipline," that is, your resistance to inertia. If you persist and push through the internal counterforces that would stand in your way of breaking through your comfort zone, you will find that in time going to the gym becomes as natural, joyful, and easy as having breakfast or going to sleep.

However, regular practice is a double-edged sword; it cuts both ways. Regular *non*-practice will take you back to the point where you began. Consistency is an infinite contiuum which points outward in two opposite directions. All Life is movement. A definition of Life could be "all that which moves." Even a stone has movement on the level of its protons, neutrons and the ever-moving electrons which whirl around them. There in no standing still – *anywhere!* You are either consistently moving and improving forward by choice, or you are consistently sliding backward and declining by default and decay.

What Consistency Is Not

I remember one time I was counseling a lady who complained to me that no matter what she had tried, she hadn't found anything that led her to the success that she so ardently desired. She continued to explain to me, "I have been trying for over 40 years, even though I haven't given up, nothing yet has worked for me, and I have set very, very high goals for myself!"

Without having to hear the gory details, i.e., complaints, of the lack of success of this lady, intuitively I understood what had to have been her problem all along. There is nothing that can convince me that if anyone who chooses and focuses on a specific goal and steadfastly continues to learn, grow, and improve along the way, even with a modicum of talent and intelligence, cannot achieve mastery of *anything* in 40 years of commitment!

If you examine closely the operative word of this lady's explanation for her continued failure, you will see the word *trying*. "Trying" is an excuse for not doing, being, and having. As the fictional character, Yoda, once said in the popular *Star Wars* movie series, "Do or do not. There is no try."

There is a huge difference between trying something and committing to something. A commitment implies consistency and persistence. Trying implies inconsistency and impatience. Consistency is not "trying something." Consistency is committing to something.

The Hummingbird Syndrome

Have you ever seen how a hummingbird moves from flower to flower. It tastes the nectar of one flower, then quickly moves on to the next and the next and the next. Many people are like this when it comes to becoming successful in any chosen endeavor. They taste or try some career or investment opportunity, however, with the first sign of setback or challenge, they throw their hands up in the air in despair and are off to trying something newer and "better." Not sticking with one thing long enough, or attempting to "commit" to too many incompatible goals at once, "spreading yourself too thin," will inevitably lead to impatience, despair, and defeat.

Consistency is Reinforced with Every Successful Repetition

Consistency is a decision that is backed by commitment and the willingness to some suffer inconvenience or discomfort along the way. Consistency involves the willingness to sacrifice the time necessary and the refusal to offer any excuses for discontinuance because the value of the prize is greater than the inertia to be ordinary.

The good news is that it gets easier and easier to be consistent. Discipline is only discipline in the beginning. However, even with this said, everyone must go through the "trial of fire" in order to prove his or her worthiness to taste the sweet nectar of success. Every time you successfully accomplish the task of this day that is part of your plan, the *resistance* to continue the next day is *weakened*. Consistency strenghtens, discipline disappears, and is replaced by joyful anticipation to continue on the upward spiral of growth and development.

You Must Know Why Your Consistency is Important

Has it become apparent now that being consistent is not for cowards or the "faint of heart?" Being consistent requires a strength of character that most people don't realize when they say that they want to do this-or-that or achieve this-or-that. If you cannot clearly see or understand why it is important to be consistent for that which you have decided to do, it is more than likely that an excuse will be found to quit or to postpone it. Again, we are talking about understanding the *why*-value.

To remain consistent, remind yourself *why* this is important. If you really want to do something you will find a way, if you don't, you'll find an excuse.

Consistency Requires an Estimated Achievement Date

Even though sometimes we must "walk by faith and not by sight," I still believe that it is a good idea to have a reasonable and approximate achievement date as we move forward to our destination. For example, if my goal is to save $24,000, and I am able to save $1000 per month, then it would be reasonable for me to project an achievement date that is approximately 24 months, or two years, from the day that I start.

If I want to get in better physical shape, depending on the level of development that I am expecting, I might set several approximate achievement dates. My first achievement date might be after 3 months, the second stage might be after 6 months, and the third stage might be after 9 months.

Consistency is predicated upon enough time for a new practice to become a habit to become a way of life, and then it becomes a natural part of your day. Setting a target date that will allow you enough time to see progress along the way, reinforces the commitment to continue.

Achievement Requires Consistency for Maintenance

Consistency is inevitable; it moves outward both ways in opposite directions of the consistency contiuum. When we set about the task to achieve a goal, we must remain consistent in order to get there. This by now, we already know. The irony, however, is that once we get there, we can *stay* there only by *remaining* consistent.

The reason for this is that life does not stand still. Life is non-stop movement in one direction or the other. We are either progressing or retrogressing. If you consistently build the trust of your spouse by consistently behaving in a trustworthy manner, this trust will not be kept by default unless you consistently *remain* trustworthy thereafter.

If you ever spend any time in a fitness gym, you will notice that those who are in the best of shape are those who appear to work out the hardest. Those who work hard to make a lot of money are usually those who work the hardest to keep and increase their money. The law is increase or decrease; nothing stands still.

It Matters Less *What* You Do and More *That* You Do

This statement may sound a little contradictory to the meaning of consistency, which is essentially the repeated practice of same time-same place. The trick is not to get too caught up in the idea of *perfect* practice versus no practice at all.

I usually get in 45 minutes of exercise on a regular daily basis, but there have been times when, due to unforeseen circumstances, I have only been able to workout 15 minutes – but I didn't skip. There have been times that my 2-pages-a-day writing schedule has been interrupted in the morning. Nevertheless, I will write a half page, if that is all I have time for.

S-happens. To skip or not to skip, that is the question. My answer is always, do what you can with what you have and the time you have available. "Skipping completely" always does more harm than good. Skipping creates a desire to skip more, and this is at a psycho-emotional level. When you skip, you bio-psychological organism believes that you are sending the message that skipping is good, and being the obedient servant that it is, will put you in the "mood" to skip more the next time. Because your bio-psychological organism is always goal-oriented, it always seeks to pursue the goal that it believes that *you* have.

By refusing to skip, by doing *something*, you break or interrupt the negative-message-pattern that skipping is good; consistency is then maintained, and the positive habit pattern remains unbroken.

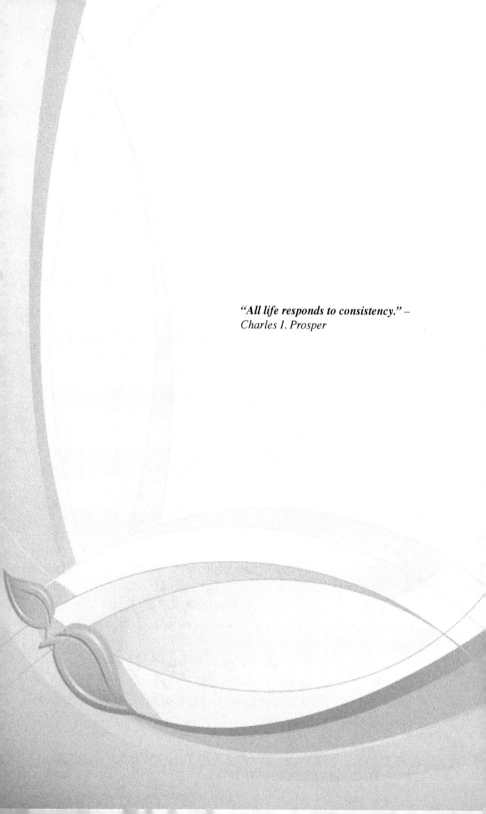

"All life responds to consistency." –
Charles I. Prosper

Why Consistency is the Secret Key to Success

Success can be defined in different ways involving different objectives. A great definition of success that I heard years ago is that success is the progressive realization of a worthy ideal or goal. So, by this definition, success does not necessarily have to involve or include money as part of the goal.

If I set out to have a successful marriage, I will consistently prove to be loyal, trustworthly, and reliable. If I want to be successful in achieving ultimate physical fitness, I will regularly eat low fat-high fiber foods, baked or broiled meat, fish and poultry, fresh fruit and vegetables, and of course exercise daily for at least 30 minutes preferably with progressive-weight resistance using barbells and dumbbells.

For purposes of this chapter, let us concern ourselves with the subject of success as money and examine how consistency is the key to success when the goal is money, wealth, and prosperity.

For many years, I was involved in and was a leader in the party balloon industry. I ran a party balloon business for more than 20 years, and I was a business consultant to hundreds of eager entrepreneurs all over the United States, Europe, Asia, and Africa. (Google "charles prosper balloons".)

Most start-up businesses fail within the first 5 years.

cording to *gallup.com,* "About 50% of new U.S. companies in their first five years. Five years of work, money, and hope – and it all just disappears, five times out of 10." (See *http://www.gallup.com/businessjournal/178787/why-new-companies-fail-during-first-five-years.aspx)*

Depending whether you are a half-glass-empty or a half-glass-full type of person, when you read this statistic, you will either be glad or depressed. If you are the half-glass-empty type of person, you will think, "Oh, my God, for every 1000 businesses that start-up in the United States, *500* will fail!" However, if you are the half-glass-full type of person, you will think, "Wow! How exciting! For every 1000 businesses that start-up in the United States, *500 will succeed!*" The group with whom you mentally and immediately identify yourself is already predicting your success. The "secret" is painfully obvious to the half-glass-full people. People don't fail, they only stop trying. People who "fail" cease to remain consistent.

Most people, in my opinion, fail with the first 5 years because they do not ask themselves, "What will I need to do to consistently produce income month-after-month?" Generally speaking, most people are not consistent, persistent, and determined to succeed. Most people, that is, the 50% who fail in the first five years, simply do not like to face unexpected challenges and to solve problems. The entrepreneurs who don't make it, give up too easy and do not remain proactive and creative problem-solvers.

The business start-ups that go south in the first five years are usually undercapitalized, that is, they start with too little capital; they simply run out of money paying overhead expenses and worker salaries, if they hire employees, before there is the chance to learn the business and discover what it takes to consistently turn a profit.

Another key element to new business success is to be surrounded by the right people. The "right" people are experts who are trained to see the blind spots of your business. These trained experts are your accountant, legal advisor, tax expert, and a successful seasoned professional who is already in the business you are in, whom you *pay* as your mentor/business consultants. These are people who I call your "accountability partners." You accountability partners will help to keep you on a consistent path to success. (More on accountability partners in a later chapter.)

How to Discover Your Life Purpose – It's Really Easy!

I have heard people ponder and stress over the question of discovering their life purpose. "I know that I am unique, and I know that I was put on this Earth to find my place in life and my special contribution, but I just don't know what it could be?"

It has been my experience that people really, truly know what it is that they are naturally attracted to. The problem is the fear of acknowledging what they already know. With knowledge or awareness comes the responsibility to do something. Awareness without immediate action becomes a form of cheap self-entertainment.

I was talking to a young man, maybe in his early twenties, in the supermarket the other day, who was helping me bag my groceries. I asked, "Jorge, do you work here full-time?" "Oh, no. I'm in school now," he replied. Curious I asked, "And what are you studying?" "I am studying veterinary." "How interesting! Do you like veterinary?" "No, not really. I would really like to be a fighter pilot in the Air Force." Bedazzled, I asked, "Then why don't you just join the Air Force and become a fighter pilot?" "Well, because my school counselor says that it would be more 'practical' to study something like veterinary since I have an affinity for animals."

At that point, I was floored by what I heard. "Doing what you love doing is the most practical thing in the world,"

I replied. "When you chose something that is practical, according to someone else's opinion, you are guaranteed to be unhappy and to fail. You fail the moment your heart is not in what you do. You are more likely to quit, by only remaining as 'practical' as possible." He nodded in agreement with an embarassed-looking smile and said, "That's true. I'm going to try to think about what you said." His statement was what I call a "definite maybe."

The irony of Jorge is that he wanted to be a fighter pilot and risk his life to protect his country, yet he was not enough of a fighter to risk his life to protect his dream. Alas, there are many people who fall into this same predicament when it comes to the discovery and pursuit of life purpose. The problem is that you choose from the head and not from the heart.

To What Have You Always Naturally Gravitated?

When people ponder over the understanding and discovery of life-purpose, I usually suggest that you look at two things: 1) natural talents and aptitude, and 2) things and activities that you have consistently gravitated toward again and again during the course of your life experience. Life purpose is not what you do; life purpose is who you are. What you do is an expression of who you are, and what you do can take form in a myriad of occupations, businesses, and/or professions.

I see myself as someone whose life purpose is to help improve the quality of life of others. This is who I am. To express myself, I could express this purpose as a teacher, social worker, writer, or public speaker, and incidentally, I have done all of these professionally at some point of life.

The key is to trust yourself and to choose for yourself, and not choose based on what your parents or teachers think that you should be or do. This is your life and your choice. Another key is not to be afraid to fail, that is, do not be afraid to miss the mark and be willing to pick yourself up, dust yourself off, and start all over again. Don't compromise. Do what you really feel and know in your heart that you must do and fulfill in your limited time on this Earth. Arnold Schwarzenegger gave his 6 secrets to success in a brilliant 4-minute YouTube video clip, which merit repeating here.

<u>Schwarzenegger's 6 Secrets of Success</u>:

1. Trust Yourself

2. Break Some Rules

3. Don't Be Afraid to Fail

4. Ignore the Naysayers

5. Work Hard

6. Give Something Back

You can view the complete YouTube clip by typing in the Search, "Arnold Schwarzenegger Motivation - 6 rules of success speech - with subtitles". However, as my 16-year-old sage daughter, Luzemily, once said, "All motivational speakers sound the same if you don't *do* anything." So again, it's not what you know, but what you consistently *do* with what you know that changes and transforms your life.

When Consistency Doesn't Work

In most cases, I would dare say that consistency is the magic bullet that will eventually produce the result of any goal that you seek. But—consistency doesn't always work. What? Yes, you read right. Consistency doesn't work when you are consistently doing the *wrong* thing, and "wrong" meaning *relative* to what you are doing and where you say you want to be. If you are in Los Angeles, California and you say that you want to go to New York, then it would be *wrong* to travel south to get there. If you are in Los Angeles and you say that you want to go to San Diego, then going south would be *right*. In terms of correct consistent action, right or wrong is relative to your goal and relative to your chosen plan of what you do, based on where you expect to be.

The success of your consistent action is predicated on the intelligence and design of your plan. Plans can change, and plans can be modified, but the initial plan must at least point clearly to the direction where you intend to be. Progress are the signposts that confirm that you are going in the right direction. Progress is the tangible result that you see, which reinforces consistency. Who wants to stop when you begin to see progress?

The rule is quite simple, if you begin to see progress and things are getting easier, and you are getting closer to your goal, you know that you are going in the *right* direction, however, conversely speaking, if things are getting more complicated, and you are getting farther and farther away from your goal, then you can be rest assured that you are going in the *wrong* direction. Consistency only works when you are consistently going in the *right* direction.

Consistency is Nothing Less than Magical

Consistency is at the core of every routine thing that we do that is important to us. We must consistently breathe in order to live. We must consistently bathe in order to remain clean. We must consistently eat every day in order to function and grow. And in my opinion, we must consistently pray, in our own way, and believe in something higher than ourselves in order to remain peaceful. Just as a perfectly straight line cannot be proven, or a perfect vacuum created, I say that perfect inertia or the complete absence of movement is another form of unprovable scientific speculation.

As we look closer at the movement of Life, we will notice that not only is all Life in constant movement, all Life is in *rhythmic* and cyclical movement. To become successful at consistency, there must be a core understanding that a rhythmical, cyclical schedule must be created. You repeat with a beat, almost in the same way that a symphony can have a complex collection of many musical instruments playing at once, yet each instrument understands its rhythmic role as part of the orchestral whole.

If you are a student and would like to earn straight A's, then I would suggest that you establish a schedule of study that would involve your studying at a certain time of day for a certain number of hours per day, ideally in the same-place environment each day. By studying in this way, instead of studying one day in the morning, and another day in the evening, where some days you would do 1 hour and other days maybe 2 and a half, it would be much more productive, for reasons of easier consistency, to establish a routine of, for example, 2 hours per day, and doing so only in the mornings.

Once you establish a clear schedule or routine for consistency to take place, life supports you and rewards you for your rhythm. Notice that after a while, you will begin to "feel like studying" when your chosen hour of study comes around. In the same way that you "feel like going to bed" once an established sleep routine has been accepted, or the same way that you "feel like eating," i.e., get hungry at a typical time of day, or you "feel like a morning jog" once jogging has become a habit. Remember, the universe rewards action, but even more importantly, the universe rewards *consistent* action.

In the beginning, there is always the resistance to change; this is part of our built in survival mechanism. What "resistance to change" attempts to do is to protect us from the unknown. The unknown can offer us rewards, but within the unknown can also lurk danger that cannot be foreseen or prepared for, even danger that could threaten our very survival. This is how our automatic built-in survival mechanism sees all change – even if it is positive change – as possible threat.

There is a way to override the fear or resistance to change by communicating to our survival mechanism that there is no danger to be concerned with. This communication can be done in one of two ways. The first way is through conscious thought or rational thinking. It is indeed possible to logically and vigorously "think through" the likelihood of any threat to survival by consciously challenging the irrational premise that all change is perilous or dangerous. The second way is through discipline. Begin your new routine, and stick with it even though "change" may feel uncomfortable until the resistance subsides and forward momentum is created. Consistency can now begin.

Consistency is How You Train Your Pet

My daughter and I have a cute 6-year-old black Chihuahua/Schipperke dog. He is Chico, our furry little family member. When we first got him at 9-months-old, he didn't know what to do or what was expected of him. So, he peed on the carpet and pooped in the corner of the kitchen. It was time to train him. Routine and consistency was key. We took him outside every morning to do his doggy business at about 6:00 a.m. and again at night at 8:00 p.m. In the first 3 weeks, he had a few "accidents." He still occassionally peed on the carpet and pooped in the corner of the kitchen, but the frequency of these accidents began to become lesser and lesser.

Somewhere around the second month, he began to look at me and whine. It was about 5:55 a.m. The consistency of the routine had taken hold, and he began to *expect* to be taken out at 6:00 a.m. Now, six years later, Chico will do whatever it takes to get my or my daughter's attention whenever he needs to go potty outside. His entire bio-psycho-organism has been conditioned and programmed, primarily through consistency to know when and how to relieve himself.

With no disrespect to the "superior species," humans are "trained" to expect certain things, for example, in a relationship through consistency as well. If your spouse has dinner ready for you every night at 6:30 p.m., and has done so over time, maybe even for many years, you learn to "get hungry" at 6:30 p.m. If you consistently put out the trash and have done so for a long period of time, by suddenly asking your significant other to do it today will cause confusion and suspicion as to why would you be requesting this.

The roles that we choose to play in a relationship are set and established through consistency. There is safety and security in consistent behavior. Knowing what to expect from others allows us to know what is permissable and how we can relate to them. Consistency defines our relationships.

The 30-Day Rule, The 60-Day Rule, and The 180-Day Rule

The question still remains, "How do we know when consistency has begun?" This is a good question, and we might want to set some arbitrary rules that can serve as the basis of an operational definition for the "beginning of consistency."

I think that once you have decided upon a plan, which involves a daily routine for the ultimate achievement of an important goal, there is a three-stage demarcation of consistency. The first stage of daily consistency can be determined when something has been done for 30 consecutive days without fail. The second stage of consistency is to continue to do the same routine until you finish doing it for a total of 60 days. The third stage of consistency is when you routinely choose to do something for 6 months, thus making it a normal part of your daily life.

There is a distinct experience at each stage, and the success of the second and third stages is predicated on the success of the first 30-day stage.

Almost anyone can be consistent on the short term, but the real magic begins when consistency is carried through repeatedly and successfully on the long term.

The 30-Day Rule of Daily Consistency (Stage 1)

In the literature of motivation and self-improvement, there is a consensus that it takes about 3 weeks for a new habit to form and set in. Generally speaking, this is true. My personal experience and that of many other people with whom I have consulted is that 30-days is a more reliable measure of seeing the first fruit of your consistent efforts. (Maybe there is some significance to the lunar cycle.)

In the first week, you can expect your most resistance to new routine. In the case of exercising, eating clean and sticking to healthy foods, or getting up an hour earlier in the morning in order to work on a new business project, or saving 10% of your income each payday, you will be amazed at all of the "reasons" or excuses your mind will offer you not to change.

In this first week, you will literally have to *force* yourself to ignore the naturally tendency to fall back to previous habits. This is the week that you will have to remind yourself of the *why.* The question becomes, "Why is the forming of this new habit so important to you?" Resistance to change weakens as you keep the importance of what you must do before you.

In addition to keeping in mind the importance of why, know also that simultaneously something else is taking place each time you successfully complete the first day, then the second day, the third, fourth, and so on until you hit the seventh day completion of your first week. Metaphorically speaking, if you see the wall of resistance as a wall, each day of completion is tantamount to poking a hole in this wall.

The result is that the wall weakens and looses structural integrity as engineers like to say. This hole punching process continues the second week, the third, and finally the fourth week of your first-month Stage 1 completion.

By the fourth week the wall has fallen, and the first surge of forward momentum is experienced. Compared to the first week, you find that there is little resistance. I say that ther is little resistance, which is to say that should you skip for two or three days immediately after your first month, if so, you will find the wall of resistance begins to build itself back up. The key is to continue and intensify the *forward* momentum.

The 60-Day Rule of Daily Consistency (Stage 2)

By the end of the 60th day or second month, the forward momentum has picked up so much until now you *want* exercise and eat clean, you *want* to get up an hour earlier in the morning to work on your new business project, and you *want* to continue saving 10% of your income each payday. With each success, your brain gives your body the command to release *endorphins* to celebrate each victory. Endorphins are the body's natural chemicals that give you the joyous "high" feeling that goes with accomplishment. The more endorphins your body produces for you, the more you want to experience. Joy is the ultimate emotion. This is the explanation of why, when the scheduled hour of your new routine comes around, you just "feel like doing it."

From this point, feeling-like-doing-it, changes to "I just can't wait to do it again!" At the second-month stage, your bio-psycho organism goes on auto-pilot. Without a second thought, you exercise and eat clean, you automatically wake up and are ready for your morning ritual, and you save 10% of your income without feeling any temptation or distraction. New habits have set in, and these new habits have become who you are. Consistency must now continue to the next stage.

The 180-Day Rule of Daily Consistency (Stage 3)

Upon having reached 6 months of consistent daily performance, your routine has been firmly established, and you are now enjoying a new way of life. "Autopilot" has set in, and the initial resistance necessitating a strong disciplined effort has long dissipated. The irony is that even though you do not have to work hard to get yourself to perform, there is now an awareness that you have to diligently work hard to *maintain* what you have achieved. To slack up and to begin skip is to go backwards and lose ground after all you have done.

You clearly realize that life does not stand still and that you must consistently *improve* in some way or the other; in truth, maintenance is a misnomer because to maintain implies an attempt to stand still, that is, to stay were you are. Internal, external, and environmental forces all have an agenda, and by default, they are attempting to move you in a *different* direction. This is the flow of life. In the absence of conscious choice, which moves you in a planned and pre-determined direction, we call the effect of the movement of these internal, external, and environmental forces "deterioration."

At the 6-month stage of progress, you will have learned the many ways that the internal, external, and environmental forces attempt to distract you off of your chosen path. You learn how to say "no" to distractions and now have the strength to stay focused on your new chosen way of life.

If you have developed the habit, for example, of getting up at 4:00 a.m. to begin your day, for whatever important ongoing project that must be done, you will have no problem or hestitation turning down an invitation to go out and party until the late hours of the night, during a weekday, when by doing so, would make the prospect of getting up early, highly unlikey and very improbable.

The 180-Day Stage of consistent progress sets the springboard for the next important developmental stage.

One Year of Consistency – the Glory Stage

Though I am attempting to create an operational definition, it can be safely said that after close to 365 days of consecutive-day consistent production, you will have reached the first period of "permanent consistency." I say this tongue-in-cheek because there is no such thing as "permanent" in the sense that there is nothing left to do. After a year of faithful practice, your routine has become a way of life. There is little or no struggle to do so as was experienced in the first few weeks. From this point onward, the second year, the third year, the fourth year, and so on root you deeper and deeper into whom you have chosen to become.

"Do what you can, with what you have, where you are." – *Theodore Roosevelt*

CHAPTER

Consistency Starts with and Important Goal

Remaining consistent and steadfast is a feat that does not happen without some strong and motivating reason to do so. There are so many enviromental factors, biological tendencies, people, and unexpected events that can and will throw us off the path if there is not a well-thought out plan and a powerful commitment to continue. In fact, remaining consistent in the real world of ongoing events is one of the most counter-intuitive human endeavors ever.

It is rather amazing, in my opinion, whenever we do find someone who is regularly and consistently pursuing a worthwhile goal. There! I've said it. I have just given you the key. There must be an important and worthwhile *goal* in order for consistency to even stand a chance.

Your important goal is the reason why you are willing to do whatever it takes in order to remain consistent. It is not even all that important to know how you will be able to succeed. It is more important to know *why* you must succeed. If the "why" is big enough, the "how" will take care of itself.

I read some time ago, a thought which summarizes well what I am trying to say here. "It you really what to do something, you'll find a way. If you don't, you'll find an excuse."

Inertia Is the First Barrier to Consistency

"An object at rest will remain at rest until acted upon by an outside force." This is Newton's First Law of Motion, which all middle-schoolers learn in the 7th and 8th grade. This is Newton's *attempt* to describe inertia. Though a better-than-nothing type of explanation of inertia, there are several fallacious assumptions inherent in Newton's First Law that makes this "law" very tenuous. First of all, complete inertia or absence of activity is unprovable.

There is constant, non-stop moment in all of Life. Even at the molecular level, there is the theoretical activity of neutrons, protons, and electrons. I think that what Newton meant to say is that when there is no *apparent* motion, an object will remain in its state of non-apparent motion until acted upon by an observable outside force. Is a flower in motion, or is it at rest? This all depends on the accessible tools of measurement and the time-factor to observe it, which will later make its movement obvious. Just because movement can't been seen or measured doesn't mean that it doesn't exist.

My point is that inertia is a state where forces are moving you in a direction which is contrary to where you would like to go. These moving forces may not be immediately observable, but they can indeed be felt, thus validating their existence. Try starting any new habit that is in stark contrast to a present habit, and you will feel this resistance. Try not eating junk food all at once, and the forces that move contrary to your changing to this new habit will begin to exert itself.

You can get the feeling that you are "stuck" where you are, therefore arising the concept of inertia. The irony of inertia is that the forces that keep inertia "in place" are everything but stable; they are dynamic and "push" in all different directions, even though this push may not be immediately observable.

So, the first barrier to becoming consistent, in a new direction, is to push *against* the forces of inertia until the inertia to stay where you are begins to weaken, thus giving way to the creation and maintenance of a new way of life.

Procrastination is the Second Barrier to Consistency

Procrastination usually happens in the beginning, once you have recognized the change that must be made. Procrastination is how inertia maintains its status quo. One misconception that I would like to dispel about procrastination is that procrastination has to do with laziness or indifference. To the contrary, the majority of people who can recognize the need for change and who make the decision to do something about it are usually far from lazy or indifferent. Procrastination has to do with fear. All change is an invitation to venture into the unknown, and on a super-subconscious self-survival level, the message of all that which is unknown is "Danger! Possible threat to survival!" So, all eagerness to get going with change is diminished. It is commonly said, "People don't like change," and now you can understand why.

The good news is that the initial resistance to change that manifests itself as the feeling of procrastination is not that difficult to reverse and to dissipate. Resistance is present, so that there will have to be *some* counter-force effort on your part. My first suggestion to overcoming procrastination is to recognize that it is a *tough* opponent but *not* an invincible one. There is the gradual approach to overcoming initial procrastination, and there is the all-on-none approach. The first approach is a little more practical for most people, while the second takes much more power of will and a higher tolerance for temporary discomfort.

Let us say that you want to get up at 5:00 a.m., and start going to the gym to workout every morning. The problem is, of course, you usually wake up at 6:00 a.m., and the idea of getting up an hour earlier seems like a monumental feat. In taking the gradual approach, you may need to prepare yourself for several days before you can accomplish this new routine. You may have to prepare your clothes before going to bed, have your meals ready for the morning, and of course begin to go to bed an hour earlier. These pre-rituals are the connected consistency events that are part of the new regime. The all-or-none approach is when you force yourself into the new routine, day after day after day in spite of everything that is going on inside, which is telling you, "You don't have to do this!" If you persist, over the course of a few days or a week, you can begin to feel the resistance of procrastination subside.

Consistency Rule #1 - Get Off Track/Get Back on Track

Consistency is an endeavor. It is an artform. It is also a dance or flow between the viscissitudes and the pull of one external distraction and another. If you are beginning in all earnest a new plan of action, which may lead you to a new way of life or important accomplishment, my suggestion is to make allowances for temporary setbacks. This is to say, that it is quite possible, for example, for you to go full steam ahead and manage to be consistent every day for 7 or 8 consecutive days in a row. Then something unexpected happens. You wake up too late. You miss your schedule to go to the gym or to write for one hour a day in the morning, or whatever your routine has been set out to be. You have gotten off track. This is "normal." The question now is "What do you plan to do when you notice that you have gotten off track?" The answer lies in following Rule #1 of Consistency. As soon as you realize you've gotten off track – *get back on track immediately!*

"S" happens! (Stuff happens :-)) There is no time to blame or berate yourself for missing, for by doing so, it is much more likely that you will start to convince yourself that your plan or your goal is impractical or "unrealistic." As soon as you miss or become inconsistent, shake it off – and begin again, as though it had never happened.

Depending on how long you had previously been doing something, it is very easy to "unconsciously" slip back into old habits. If, for example, you skip a new routine for 3 or 4 days in a row, it is very likely that you will slip back into old ways. Even if you "snap out of it" and realize what has happened after a week of inactivity, you must begin again as though the inactivity had never happened.

The greatest allay to consistency is the power of persistence. Unexpected events are out of your control, but persistence is totally within your control. The dynamic which drives persistence is the power of free will. Persistence is predicated on the power of an individual to decide whom he or she chooses to be *this day*. No matter what happened yesterday or the day before, what matters only is whom do you choose to be and what do you choose to do *this day!* If you get off track, get back on track immediately, and begin again. The quicker you get back on track, the less likely it becomes that you will get off track any time again soon.

Partial Consistency Is Better Than Zero Consistency

If something unexpected interferes with full completion of a regular task that you have set out to do, do *some* of it, if that is all that is possible at that time. Perfectionism is the plight of consistent action over time. I say over time because sooner or later perfect practice will not be feasible on some occasions. The idea of course is to be as complete as possible in what you must do, but life happens. I love to use examples of how I remain consistent in going to the gym at 4:20 a.m. There have been times when unexpected morning events have made me go to the gym at 5:30 a.m. instead of my regular 4:20 a.m. This would mean that a complete 45-minute to an hour workout would not be possible. So, should the decision in this case be all or none? If I can't workout for an hour, should I just skip today and begin again tomorrow? In cases, such as these, I will do as many minutes that I can. But I won't skip. If I can do only 20 minutes, I will do only 20 minutes. If I can do only 10 minutes, ten minutes I will do. But I just won't skip.

The principle of partial consistency, whenever necessary, can be applied to any regular routine that you have set. You save $500 a month as part of your real estate investment account, with a goal of saving $20,000 for the next 40 months. For 10 months straight, you have managed to put away your $500 per month. On the 11th month, you can only deposit $300. Then you deposit, $300 on the 11th month, and resume at $520 a month for the next 10 months until you can comfortably resume at the $500 a month consistency schedule.

You are writing a book, and your schedule is one hour a day at 5:30 a.m. Everyday for several months, you have consistently written for an hour a day at 5:30 a.m. You get an unexpected phone call. Now you can only write for 20 minutes. Write those 20 minutes diligently, and resume your regular one hour of morning writing on the next day.

Partial is better than perfect.

Inconsistent with Minor Details But Not the Overall Plan

You may be occasionally inconsistent with the details of your plan, but you are never allowed to be inconsistent with the execution of the plan itself.

When it comes to working out, I get the best workout when I go to *24-Hour Fitness,* which is only a 7 to 10-minute drive from where I live. There is a great variety of weights and exercise machines, and to be submerged in the total atmosphere of fitness, surrounded by other enthusiasts of bodybuilding keeps my motivation high. There are, however, the occasional times, not often but ocasional, when it is not feasible for me to drive to the gym. So, what do I do on these occasions? On these times, I will do what I can do. I will go to my living room and do 40 minutes of push-ups for my shoulders and triceps, chin-ups for my biceps and back, leg lunges with my hands at my side for my frontal thighs, and leg raises and situps on the floor for my abdominals. Skipping is never an option.

Small But Consistent Is Better Than Big and Sporadic

You cannot "make up" for lost time when it comes to consistency. You can only begin again on the next opportunity. Let us say that I am to exercise everyday for 30 minutes, and I skip 4 days in a row. (This is just a supposition.) On the fifth day, attempting to workout for 2 hours will not make up the lost 30 minutes a day of the last four days. If I have begun a savings plan of $100 a month, and I omit saving for three consecutive months, placing $400 in my account in the fifth month is not the same as saving $100 for three consecutive months and then placing $400 in my account in the fourth month. Four months saving in the first scenario would be $400. Four months of consistent saving in the second scenario would result in $800.

Each day of lost opportunity is lost forever. You can begin again, but you can never recover a day that you have squandered. Each day counts, which is why you must make it count.

Could a drop of water split a mountain in two? The answer is yes, but with a little thought and reflection, it would not take one drop but rather many drops, one after another, consistently over time. The principle of an ultimate effect is "small but repetitive." I once witnessed a very interesting result of a small but repetitive action, which took place after about two months. I was the mentor of Alex, a young man, age 15, whom accompanied me to a neighborhood fitness center, where I trained him on the use of free weights and exercise equipment. We trained about 5 days a week. After a vigorous workout, we would go to the men's locker room, shower, and dress. Alex had this routine where he would come out of the shower with a towel wrapped around his waist, go to a mirror, and wet a small black plastic comb under the water faucet, then tap his comb three times on the edge of the face bowl counter to shake off the excess water, and comb his hair to one side. This he did every day of the five days a week we worked out. He would wet the comb, then tap the comb three times on its back edge to shake off the excess water, and comb his hair to one side. Then one day, after about two months of this regular grooming routine, when he started tapping the comb in order to shake of the water – after the second tap – the comb *split* perfectly in two! The split was so straight and perfect, it looked as though it had been cut by a precision saw. When I saw this, I realized that I had witness something that demonstrated a very powerful principle and secret. Every repetition of consistency creates an effect, even if it cannot be readily perceived by the human eye or the other senses.

A what point, does consistency create a result? Answer: Immediately. Existence of "what is" is not predicated on one's perception of it. There are many things that exist totally independent of our perception of them. Radio waves are all-pervading in the room where you are right now, even though you cannot perceive them. The proof of this becomes obvious the moment you turn on a radio capable of capturing and transmitting them to the human ear, which they can then be perceived and their existence is validated.

Consistency creates a result from the *first* repetition. Results are progressive and cumulative until ordinary things consistently done produce extraordinary results that can be seen.

Consistency Creates Critical Mass

Consistency creates critical mass. In other words, at what point do thoughts become things? At what point does a grain of sand become a beach? At what point do drops of water become an ocean? At what point does consistent love become trust? All consistency reaches its point of critical mass. At what point critical mass will be reached cannot always be predicted in terms of timeframe, however, critical mass is *guaranteed* as long as you remain consistent.

Consistency Is Always a Conscious Choice

The effect of consistency over time can never be underestimated. Consistency is not automatic or "natural" for most human beings. In fact, consistency is one of the most unnatural acts of all human behavior. Consistency requires effort. Choosing requires effort. And what's more, consistency requires choosing daily, that is, today, and again tomorrow, the next day, the next, and the next. You choose today, and you must choose the same again tomorrow.

It is also important to keep in mind that consistency is the repetition of *simple*, ordinary things, which produce extraordinary results. Like the saying goes, "It's the little things that count." Luzemily, my 16-year-old daughter was on summer vacation. When we were having breakfast she admitted to me that she had watched way too much television the day before, maybe about 4 hours straight. Without me having to admonish her, and on her own accord, she told me that this would not happen again. "I'm sorry dad. I really know better. I was consistently watching way too much TV yesterday." I said, "You were not watching consistently, you were watching *excessively*. There is a difference." Since she knew a philosphical discussion was about to start, so, her quick reply was, "Well, is it possible for someone to do something consistently excessive?" "Yes," I replied, "but consistent excessiveness is the definition of self-destruction."

When we look at the most impressive results of consistent action over time, we will usually observe the the consistent actions were usually very simple, basic, and unimpressive. If we examine the creation of any animal or plant, we will always see that within each of these living structures there are smaller elements of which they are composed, which had to consistently grow over time. All plants and animals started out as small and simple cells, which gradually yet consistently reproduced itself over time until its final goal was reached.

Greater Commitment Leads to Greater Consistency

The success of consistency is predicated on commitment, and commitment is triggered by a conscious realization of the value or importance of the goal that is sought. There are no shortcuts to consistency. Consistency is always the long winding road. This reminds me of a supervisor at a job where I worked as a social worker, who told me that he wanted to learn to speak Spanish. Knowing that I am fluent in Spanish and that I taught Spanish in the high schools here in Los Angeles for many years, he asked my advice on the best program that he should purchase in order to learn it. My answer to this question is as always, "It doesn't really matter what language system that you choose to learn Spanish. If it has been proven to work, all of them are good. It is really about your commitment and consistency to study and practice." "I heard that the Rosetta Stone program for learning Spanish was very good," he said. "Yes, Rosetta Stone is very good, and it is also the priciest," I answered. "It can be as high as $500." "I don't mind paying the price. I would really like to learn it. I don't really need to be fluent. Just holding a conversation would be enough."

What I observed was a commitment to pay a high price as a tacit trade-off for lack of strong commitment to mastery. What I have observed is that in many cases where personal achievement of some sort is the objective, a person will spend a whole lot of money for a program, system, or package with the unconscious premise that the more money spent will be equivalent to a higher likelihood of success when there is little or no serious commitment. To the contrary, it has been my observation and experience that the more the person spends on a package or program, the less likely he will be consistent. You see this all of the time. A late night "coach potato" decides that it is time to lose a few extra pounds. A informerical appears offering a new 21st century piece of exercise equipment promising to melt inches of fat off of your thighs and waistline – for only six easy payments of $199, or something like that. That person puts down his bag of chips, grabs his credit card, calls the 800 number and places the order. Well, we know how the story usually goes. The miracle equipment arises, and fast forward fives months, and the miracle equipment is gathering dust in the garage. I have seen committed and consistent people lose weight and develop very beautiful bodies with little or no fancy equipment. I have seen people achieve their fitness goals with clean and healthy eating combined with a simple but consistent regimen of push-ups, chin-ups, leg lunges, sit-ups, leg-raises, and 30 minutes of jogging five times a week upon awakening.

Oh, and you may be wondering what happen with the supervisor who wanted to learn Spanish. He did order the most expensive version of the Rosetta Stone program, and he did begin and practice with it for about two weeks. Nine months later, I asked, "How's it going with your Spanish program?" "Well, I need to get back with it again. Once I get a little more time, I will begin again." More time is an illusion and does not come by default . We all have the same 24 hours in a day. We make time for that which we deem important.

Consistency requires sacrifice, sacrifice that is renewed on a daily basis. The power of consistency is predicated on harnessing and accessing the power within each individual to succeed no matter what. Consistency is a tool just as a saw is a tool. A saw does not work until you work it, and consistency does not work until you work it – *consistently.*

Remembering Your Goal Fuels Consistency

Many years ago, I was in Gold's Gym of Venice Beach, CA, and I was privy to have the opportunity to have a conversation with former Mr. America and well-known bodybuilder Jim Morris, now 79 on the subject of motivation. I remember that I said, "I plan to always stay motivated." I will never forget his answer, "Goals create motivation." To this I agree, and I would add *important* goals will create greater motivation. The more important the goal, the greater the motivation. Then, I say, if you can keep your goal in the forefront of your consciousness, continued motivation with the persistence to back it up is virtually guaranteed.

Remember the *why* of a new and challenging goal is particularly important in the beginning stages, when you are in the process of disciplining yourself and making it into a habit.

Some goals have a built-in memory system and an automatic pilot set up shortly after starting. The fear of loss or the fear of poverty can motivate consistency in the beginning. Fear, in my opinion, is not the best source of motivation in the long run, but initially it can wake you up from upcoming or impending disaster. Planning and saving for retirement is often not one of those things that most young people worry about. The few wise and lucky young people who start retirement planning and savings early, can prepare themselves for a bright and prosperous future in their later years. But what makes something like saving for retirement difficult for most people is that one, they don't see it as important yet, and two, if they do see it as important and begin at, say, 30 or 40 years old, the biggest problem is to remain *consistent* for the next 25 or 35 years. What makes retirement planning and savings work is consistency, and as I hope it is understood at this point, consistency cannot be taken for granted. Consistency does not happen by default. It takes a concerted, determined, and planned daily effort to achieve consistency and maintain it.

Consistency Requires a Day-By-Day Commitment

We hear about people who renew their marriage vows every 10 years, and I think that this is a beautiful thing. We have to do something similar to renewing our marriage vows. We have to renew our vows to remain consistent on a daily basis. Every day counts, and there is no such thing as missing a day and "making it up" the next day. It is impossible to make a missed day up because the day missed is gone; what you do today is not the same day as the day that was missed. True, you are starting a new day, but you can never *replace* a day that was missed because it is not the same day. This is the same concept when people believe that if they are saving money that they can borrow money from themselves and pay it back the next month. You cannot replace money that you've borrowed from yourself because *it is not the same money.* The money that you borrowed is no longer there just as the day you miss is gone forever; it cannot be pulled back from time and replaced.

Renew commitment, and make every day count.

"The universe likes consistency." – *Jennifer Urezzio*

Routine Makes Consistency Possible

There are some things that make consistency possible and increase the probability that you will not falter and fall off the path. One of the things that will make consistency easier is to establish a routine to follow. The very definition of consistency is conformity with previous practice. Therefore, it can be said that, routine creates consistency and defines consistency at the same time.

The Holy Bible puts the importance of routine in this way in *Ecclesiastes, chapter 3*, verses 1 through 8:

1 To every *thing there is* a season, and a time to every purpose under the heaven:

2 A time to be born, and a time to die; a time to plant, and a time to pluck up *that which is* planted;

3 A time to kill, and a time to heal; a time to break down, and a time to build up;

4 A time to weep, and a time to laugh; a time to mourn, and a time to dance;

5 A time to cast away stones, and a time to gather stones together; a time to embrace, and a time to refrain from embracing;

6 A time to get, and a time to lose; a time to keep, and a time to cast away;

7 A time to rend, and a time to sew; a time to keep silence, and a time to speak;

8 A time to love, and a time to hate; a time of war, and a time of peace.

Once a routine or regular schedule has been set and you have begun to practice it successfully, it naturally becomes *the time* for that activity. I have noticed that if I have set up a routine to write at 3:30 a.m. every morning for an hour, it is easier to write in that early morning hour that trying to write later in the day at 3:30 p.m. for an hour. The sudden change in time becomes a struggle in that it "doesn't *feel* like the 'right' time." You eat breakfast in the morning and dinner in the evening. You go to bed at night, and wake up in the morning. Rhythm and routine is the only way the universe can exist. Many things must move, and in order for many things to move in different directions at once, there must be harmony, rhythm, or routine.

"Same-Time Same-Place" Makes a Successful Routine

I have found that there are two key elements to making a successful routine. These two key elements are to create the routine based on an activity or practice that takes place at the same time and the same place. This is the ideal situation for successful consistency. True, there will be times when it is not feasible or practical to do what you must do at the same time or at the same place, but the more times you can do what you must do at the same time and the same place, the higher is the probably that you will stay on track and with the least amount of effort.

In time, the specific hour that you choose to practice becomes your "hour of persistence-power," and the specific place that you choose to practice becomes a "place of persistence-power." The time and the place you honor will soon honor and support you. When the time comes and you go to the *place*, without knowing or understanding why, you just *feel* like doing it.

A Routine Evolves from a Well-Thought-Out Plan

Before we can commit to a plan of action in order for it to eventually become a routine, it behooves us to choose wisely. Choosing a plan to which to commit is much like choosing a life partner. First, it is of paramount importance to understand exactly where it is that we want to go and what it is that we want to achieve. Upon achieving our objective, what would it look like, and what would it feel like? What is it that we can see ourselves doing? With whom do we see ourselves surrounded enjoying this accomplishment with us? Based on the desired experiences that we seek, a plan of action is created.

Plans may have to be researched and professionals, experienced with your field of endeavor, may need to be consulted. However, after all has been said and done, you will ultimately have to be the one to decide and commit to any chosen plan of action. If any advice goes contrary to your common sense, the rule is trust your intuition before trusting the "experts."

In the beginning stages of the execution of a new plan, it will be necessary to monitor its effectiveness. Do you see it bringing you closer to your goal, or does it feel counter-intuitive to what you are trying to do? When I first decided to commit to getting in top physical shape, I enrolled in my neighborhood fitness center, and I planned get home from work, and be to the gym by 6:00 p.m. This was not a feasible plan because by the time I finished, it was 7:00 p.m., and by the time I got home it was 7:30 p.m. Preparing and serving dinner for my daughter would be 8:30 p.m., which was very late for a school night. So, I had to revamp my plan. I realize that the *best* time for exercising would have to be at 4:20 a.m. I initially resisted the thought, but after serious consideration, I could see that this was the absolute the best time. I went to bed by 8:30 p.m., and after 3 weeks of commitment, what had been a struggle at first became a routine as natural and as easy as I had previously gotten up at 6:30 a.m. I became consistent, and I began to see the results that I wanted. This was the plan that worked.

Create a Routine Tailor-Made to Your Situation

When it comes to creating your success routine leading to the fulfillment of your goal, be careful about following formula-type routines that were originally designed for someone else's different and unique situation or idiosynchatric personality type. I remember when I first decided to go back to the gym, I hired a fanatical fitness guru. Keep in mind that I had not regularly been exercising for a couple of years, and I had gotten quite out of shape. His advice from my first day was, "I want you to do 200 push-ups and 100 sit-ups." I said, *"Whaat!"* "Yeah, no matter what, do whatever it takes to do those push-ups and sit-ups – every day for the first week." His training philosophy was something like, "If I haven't made you throw-up yet, I want you to do more!" Long story short, I fired him, and I designed a *sane* and gradual routine of progressive weight resistance that has been giving me satisfying and positive results even since.

Experiment with Routine Until One Fits You

The routine to which you commit must be selected to fit your particular situation, personality, and personal goals. This may involve some trial and error initially in the same way that you select a new pair of shoes. You don't want anything that is too tight nor do you want anything that is too loose. You don't want any hand-me-down routine from someone else's particular situation or circumstance. Your routine is as personal as the toothbrush you use. It cannot be for anybody else. Your routine must be you, and it must be new.

Routine Creates Habit and Habit Becomes Consistency

The natural concomitant of routine is that, as you persist, the routine becomes a habit. *Webster's New World Dictionary,* 2003, page 290, defines **hab-it** as "a thing done often and, hence, easily." So, as we examine this definition, we see the essence of how a habit is created and the positive result of doing so. A thing must be done *often...* And so what is "often?" *Webster's New World Dictionary,* 2003, page 449, defines **of-ten** as "many times; frequently." When *Webster* says a "thing," it appears to me that it is not referring to "one thing and then another." It appears to me that the thing it is referring to is the *same* thing, which is done many times. To do something "many times" is relative, but one thing is for certain, we are not talking about once or twice then quitting. Many times indicates *repeatedly.* Therefore, if some thing is done repeatedly, that is, many times, it eventually becomes easier to do. When something becomes easier to do, there is less conscious effort.

From Conscious Effort to Autopilot

The universe rewards action, and the universe reinforces repeated consistent action. Your ability to do a repeated action strenghtens with each repetition. With enough frequency, what starts out as conscious effort, becomes automatic action requiring little or minimal conscious effort, other than the awareness that it is time to do the chosen action. The positive result of routine is that it moves you from the initial stage of conscious effort to an eventual stage "autopilot." With all change, there is some initial resistance. Our psycho-biological organism is not too keen on change because with change, there is uncertainty, and with uncertainty, there is the possibility of danger, and with the possibility of danger, there exists the ultimate threat, which is the cessation of our existence, i.e., death. Once our psycho-biological organism sees that the repeated activity poses no threat, it thus cooperates and makes the repeated activity easier to do because our psycho-biological organism is also our servo-mechanism, it is our "genie in the bottle." Our wish is its command, as long as the wish has been screened out through repeated trials, excluding the possibility of danger.

Consistency is Measured by Progress

So, let us say that we have managed to be consistent in doing a plan that has been designed to lead us to a certain goal. What is the point of consistently doing anything if it is not taking us closer to the desired objective? The only justification for persistence is progress. Progress is the greatest reinforcer for consistency, and progress fuels persistence. As we see ourselves improving and getting closer to our goal, we want to continue and do more. Seeing progress gives us that shot of happy chemicals called endorphins, which course through our body.

Inches can be measured by rulers or yardsticks. Bodyweight can be measured by a bathroom scale. Temperature can be measured by a thermometer, and a student's understanding of a subject can be measured by a grading system. All tools of measurement are a convention, which appears to give the information needed regarding some change. In order to experience the thrill of progress and to keep determination and commitment alive, progressive signposts must be designated. The only one who can determine progress that is based on a personal goal is you. You must know what your accomplished goal looks and feels like as well as understand what progress toward the goal looks and feels like. Progress need not always be pleasant, but it needs to be recognized. For example, when you begin weight training and wake up sore the next day, this is a sign of progress because in order for new muscle tissue to develop, the weak and worn out muscle tissue must be broken down and washed away, making way for the development of bigger and stronger muscles. One of the clearest and most recognizable signpost of progress is that the task that is part of the plan of action becomes easier and easier to execute. The initial inertia and resistance to change begins to wane. Once initial resistance begins to wane, the desire to do more is strenghtened, which is followed by an eagerness to continue and to never skip.

Progress Is Like a Lightning Bolt and Not a Straight Line

When it comes to seeing progress, it must be understood that progress moves at an angle from bottom up, and not in a straight line, but more like a lightning bolt. First of all, as we have observed previously, there is no such thing as a perfectly straight line; there will always be some deviation as the line stretches outward. A line cannot be stable because the molecules that would compose any line are not stable by definition because all life is movement. Progress happens like a jagged cliff with its peaks and valleys and its ups and downs, much like the way a lightning bolt stretches across the sky from a cloud to the earth. As we progress toward our goal, there will be good days and other days not as good; there will be high energy days and low energy days. Good days, "bad" days, the important thing is that we have *days*. Sooner or later we will run out of them, so it is best to make the most of each of them as they are given to us, and keep on keeping on.

"Luck is a factor of what I do or I fail to do in a timely and consistent manner." – *Charles I. Prosper*

Who Is Your Accountability Partner?

Do you have consistency reminders? Consistency reminders can be specially made motivational message notes that can be ordered from any printing service, which have a soft plastic back that are removable magnets, which can be placed on your refrigerator door, something you will see on a daily basis. You can put similar notes on your bathroom mirror, so that every time you shave, wash your face, brush your teeth, or put on makeup, you will be reminded of what you must do. Screensaver notes on your computer screen or colorful message notes laminated and used as bookmarks will also serve you greatly to keep your mind focused on the task ahead. All of these consistency reminders are not to be overlooked; you need all the help you can get. However, one of the greatest assets in your corner by far is your accountability partner.

Do you have an accountability partner? Have you even considered an accountability partner? They are not to be underestimated. Chosen wisely, an accountability partner can be the marginal difference between success and failure. Help is all around us. I do not mean this figuratively; I mean this literally. Help is synonymous to opportunity. Opportunity exists all around us, and the ability to see opportunity is predicated on our willingness to see it. Help can be seen the moment we are willing to see it and to take advantage of it.

Accountability Partners Help You to Remain Consistent

Very few of us in life reach any important long term goal alone. Because consistency is one of the biggest and most underestimated challenges which is taken for granted, we need all the help we can get. An accountability partner can keep you focused, clear, and motivated as to the why and the how of what you need to do and continue doing. But great care must be taken in the selection of your accountability partner. So, how is an accountability partner selected? I would say that the person or persons whom you select has the knowledge and experience pertaining to your goal and he or she is someone who has your best interest at heart.

If I want to invest in real estate and become successful with this long term goal, I would *not* ask a colleague at work, who has rented his or her whole life, who owns no property and has never successfully invested in anything, someone who has only real books on real estate and one who only *knows* of someone else who has successfully invested in real estate. I would only hire an experienced real estate investor, who has a long track record of successful investments, someone who knows *how* to be consistent and with *what*.

There are two problems in utilizing an inexperienced or unknowledgeable accountability partner. One, it is quite possible that the person you have enlisted to "help" you secretly envies your ambition and may unwittingly sabotage your efforts by giving you the wrong advice, and thus maliciously steering you in the wrong directions, and two, for lack of the proper knowledge and experience, the wrong accountability partner is most likely to give you the wrong advice, not intentionally, but out of ignorance of exactly what it would take to remain consistent by doing the right things, those things proven to lead you to where you want to go.

Announce Your Goal to a Trusted Confidant

There are some cases where you can announce some goals to a loved-one or trusted confidant who can help you stay on course without knowing exactly everything that you have to do. When I told my daughter that I had made a decision to get up every morning by 4:20 a.m. and go to the gym, *she was on it!* The first few days of this new goal were the hardest. I got up, and I struggled. Somewhere around the 14th day, my alarm didn't go off. I suspect that my daughter noticed that I hadn't gotten up because she can hear me move around and stir from the next room. *"Ding! Ding! Ding!"* was the soft sound of the chime notes that I received in a text from my iPhone next to my bed. I slowly opened my eyes, turned to the side and read the text – not knowing who could be texting me at this pre-dawn hour. "Get up dad!!!!! And work out!!!!!!!..." I then realized that my fitness goal was important to her as well. I got up and went to the gym. In the following days to come, it was not difficult to get up because I knew how much taking care of myself meant to my daughter.

Join a Club or Association of Like-Minded People

A club or association is a built-in group of accountability partners, who oftentimes have the knowledge and experience to guide you and keep you on the right track. If you are a first-time real estate investor, for example, it would be a great move to join your local Apartment Owners Association. Within this group, you will find seasoned and beginning investors, such as yourself. Within this group, it would be quite simple to find a mentor to guide you through the learning curve of investing. The interesting thing about being part of a club or association of like-minded people is that every time you meet, you are given a new surge of interest and determination. One of the most classic and time-tested associations for keeping one on the right path is your local church or other place of worship.

Assuming that you choose your group or association wisely, based on the goals that you have set and the likelihood that your chosen group has the people with the knowledge and experience to guide you, you are more likely to persist and persist with greater enthusiam. Sometimes something as simple as joining a fitness club, going there everyday on a regular basis, and seeing other dedicated members will help. I remember one morning, when I checked in to workout, the guy who signed me up, greeted me at the sign-in counter with a smile and said, "Wow! I notice that you have been coming in every day now. Congratulations. That's great!" Just this simple comment gave me that little extra boost of pride, which made me eager to stay even more consistent; he became an accountability partner by default.

Set Up a Support Group and Meet Regularly

In some cases, you can set up and create your own group surrounding a topic on which each member has a passion. I remember when I set up my first Focus Success Group. A small but very intense group of us met once a month, facilitated by me, in the recreation room of the apartment village where I lived. Our purpose was to set our most important goals and share them with the group. We encouraged and supported each other to make a plan and take immediate action with our goals. Members of the group would then report back on following meetings and share the successes of their efforts. Suggestions of specifically what *should be* done was kept to a minimum. The key focus was to encourage eachother to continue moving forward and to do whatever it took to discover the next and the next step to take. Support groups are a haven of accountability partners.

Team Up with Someone Who Has the Same Goal

Teaming up with someone who has the same goal can be a good

or a bad idea depending on the situation and how it is set up. Because I am fluent in Spanish and am a former Spanish high school teacher, it is not uncommon for people to come up and ask me for advice in learning Spanish. Once I was approached by a work colleague who told me that he had purchased a very good Spanish program, I said, "That's fine, however, the secret to language mastery is to have a proven system or program for learning grammar or sentence structure, and then the practice of the new language must be environmentally reinforced, that is, ideally you should be in an enviroment where you have the opportunity to practice daily." He replied, "Well, I have a friend who wants to practice Spanish with me." "Does he have native ability?" I ask. "No, he is learning it just like me." I explained that this plan for language mastery is questionable; it is more like the blind leading the blind. In the case of learning language, an accountability partner would better be a person with native fluency, otherwise, the chance is that he could be learning the poor pronunciation or incorrect sentence structure of the other.

There are those cases, however, where what you do is not predicated on the knowledge of the other. Take the example of working out in the gym. If you have initially been trained properly and know what it is that you have to do, you can team up with a training partner, who has an equivalent understanding and knowledge of exercise. The idea is to regularly meet at the same time and place to workout together and keep each other consistent and motivated.

I remember one time, I had a friend, who was my morning jogging partner. No matter what, at 5:00 a.m., there he was knocking on my door. There was no way I was going to miss. How can you make excuses to someone who is consistent and taking the trouble of helping you out? You have dual motivation, you don't want to disappoint the other person or yourself.

Hire a Professional Consultant

Sometimes finding an accountability partner may come at a price, and that is okay as long as you are saving time by avoiding unnecessary and costly mistakes.

It amazes me how often budding entrepreneurs catch the fire of starting their own business yet overlook the importance of hiring professional consultants to guide them in the right directions and to keep them motivated as they encounter the unexpected obstacles that are guaranteed to show up.

When I decided to begin my real estate investment strategy, I didn't just depend upon my own research and the real estate books I had read, I hired one of the sharpest realtors and real estate investors in Los Angeles, California with over 30 years experience of doing and practicing what he preaches. When I want to avoid paying excessive taxes for my higher income, I consult my real estate tax accountant, and for writing up contracts, I hire my real estate attorney, who specializes in contract writing.

When I decided to discover the best ways to market and promote my books, I didn't try to figure it all out soley through personal study and trial and error. I hired an experienced book marketing consultant, who has helped over 400 authors and publishers sell more books and spread their message like wildfire.

When I first decided to get into seriously good physical shape, I did my homework and I studied the best books on the subject of fitness and bodybuilding, and then I hired a professional contest-winner bodybuilder to design my workouts, counsel me on how to eat, and to train me in my first 6 months.

The advice and guidance that a professional consultant offers you far outweighs the money investment to have him or her in your corner. You shorten the learning curve and you save money that might have been poorly spent by trying to figure it out all on your own.

Pay a Counselor (Psychological Issues)

Let us say that you have personal, emotional, or marital problems. You have three choices: 1) You can try to solve your problems on your own, 2) you can get advice from a friend or relative, or 3) you can hire a professional counselor. When you have personal or psychological issues, attempting to solve the problem on your own has built-in disadvantages in that you are too close to the situation, usually, in order to look at it objectively and creatively and come up with positive alternatives. I am not saying that it is impossible to take on personal problems without the help of third parties, it is just an uphill struggle. Getting advice from a friend or relative can be helpful, or it can make matters worse. If the friend's or relative's perspective is negative, one that is lacking in lucid thinking, you may get an opinion, but that is not the same thing as good advice. In many cases, the best way to go is to avoid flying solo or getting advice from a well-intentioned but misinformed friend or relative, is to seek out an accountability partner in the form of a professional counselor. Therapists are also an option, but picking a therapist should be done carefully by first understanding what type of therapy is being used and how it is likely to help the problem that you are attempting to solve. I have a masters in psychology, having graduated with a specialty in marriage and family therapy, and in my opinion, cognitive behavioral therapy, especially rational-emotive therapy as founded by the late Dr. Albert Ellis is among the best of therapeutic approaches. You can type in "cognitive behavioral therapy, your city" in the Google search bar to locate a qualified therapist in your area. Be careful with psychiatrists; their approach is strongly pharmacological, this is to say that psychiatrists like to drug you with prescription medication in order to get a hold of your problem or situation.

See Your Doctor (Medical Issues)

One of the most well-known of accountability partners for health and medical problems is your family physician or medical specialist. There comes a time when home remedies and "natural cures" that you discover on a highly viewed YouTube clip should be circumvented for a visit to your medical doctor. A good doctor will not only be able to tell you exactly what is wrong, in most cases, she will give you a course of action, along with follow up visits. A good hospital or clinic can be one of the best accountability partners. At this moment, I remember that I was given a called, *for the 4th time,* from Kaiser Permanente Hospital of Los Angeles that I am due for my colo-rectal screening – something that I have been procrastinating and putting off for some time. Hmmm. Since I am writing this chapter, I guess it is my sign that I should make my appointment and go in for the screening. I guess accountability partners do work!

Talk to Your Minister (Spiritual Issues)

Sometimes psychological and spiritual issues may overlap, but in many cases, your accoutability partner for decisions of morals and ethics may fall into the domain of consulting with your minister, rabbi, or priest. For a classic example, if you are a married person, with a loving spouse and devoted family, and you are involved in a torrid extramarital relationship, with someone other than a spouse, your spiritual counselor may be the one to help you see the possible consequences before the course of your actions happen to blow up in your face.

Be Open-Minded and Accept Their Feedback

The whole point of an accountability partner is to help to keep you on track and to help you to see your blind spots. Can you look at the back of your head right now, without a mirror? You can't, but a friend or loved-one could easily do that for you because they are in a position to see behind your field of vision. This is how accountability partners work, they encourage you to stay on the right track, and they can see things from a vantage point that you cannot. Most important of all, listen to their feedback with an open mind, and take action by following their advice when it resonates with you and your common sense.

"A man that shows a woman consistency will never have to worry about her loyalty."
– *Anonymous*

CHAPTER

Consistency—the Key to Successful Relationships

We may fall in love with someone for their beauty, wit, charm or intellect, but we *stay* in love with them because of their consistency to keep giving and showing the same things that attracted us in the first place. That which all of us want from those whom we love the most is to know that they are always there for us when everyone else is no where to be found. We have that special feeling that our loved-ones have "got our backs." When we can tell a person, "You're always there for me," in essence we are saying "I can depend on you," and to depend on someone means that they have had a consistent "track record" for being the same in personality and in character. With a person who is consistent in his or her behavior, there is no confusion as to the nature of your relationship with them. When a person shows consistent behavior, be it positive or negative, it allows you the opportunity to choose or not to choose to have that person as part of your life.

In the case of a work situation or environment, you may or may not have the choice to minimize contact with a particular co-worker who is consistently negative and difficult to be around, but at least you can discern the difference between a "friend" and a work colleague and relate to that individual accordingly. By the fruit, i.e., consistent behavior, we can know the tree, i.e, the person.

Consistency = Trust

I was going to begin this section about consistency and trust in interpersonal human relationships, but the first thing that popped into my mind was *Amazon.com*. I order a lot from *Amazon*: books, equipment, furniture, you name it. *Amazon* is one of the largest retail providers of a limitless variety of every type of item imaginable. If what you want exists and is for sale, it is likely *Amazon* can ship it to you. I then asked myself, how is it that *Amazon* grew from an online company providing only books to become a mega-giant fulfilling consumer desires all over the world? If you have ever placed an order with *Amazon*, and they give you an estimated delivery date, your product will usually arrive a day or two earlier. If you order same-day deliver, your product comes *same day*. I have been using this service for well over 10 years, and I have *never* been disappointed. Because they consistently deliver and do what they promise, I have learned to trust them. This trust was built over time, thus the formula is simple: *Consistency + Time = Trust*.

It is true that trust in another does not happen over night, but given enough time, it will happen if you keep in mind that consistency is the key. Let's say you meet someone new and then you go out on these incredibly romantic dates of fine wine, dining, dancing, and barefeet walks along sandy beaches at sunset. You feel waves wash up to your ankles and tickle playfully between your toes; these are fun and enjoyable moments. However, for serious, fulfilling, and long-term love relationships, it is not just the "romantic person" you must get to know, it is the "consistent" person you must get to know in all other important aspects of your relationship. What good is a romantic person if they consistently break their promises? What price romance if the other person occasionally lies and attempts to use romance to assuage the situation? A person who is consistently honest, patient, understanding, forgiving, dependable, and kind, and who has demonstrated this unchangeably over time, will be of much more value that he or she who attempts to rest the relationship entirely on the thin paper of romance. *Consistency + Time = Trust.*

Consistency Has to Do with Reliability

Consistent good behavior, when it has to do with relationships, is so important because consistent good behavior means that there is reliability. If there is reliability, there is certainty. If there is certainty, there is trust. If there is trust, there can be love. Essentially, what is reliability? Reliability is doing what you promise to do or what you say you will do. And let's set the records clear; whatever you say you will do is a promise, whether you say the words "I promise" or not. My mother, may she rest in peace, gave me a long time ago one of the best defintions of success that I have ever heard; she said, "Success is doing what you say you will do." Success is self-reliance. Success is keeping the promises you make to yourself. If you "keep promises" to yourself and others, we will find that consistent positive and productive behavior has got to be part of this success formula.

Placed on my desk in front of me, as I type these words, I see the reverse side of a dollar bill of the United States of America. On the back and in the center it says, as it does on all U.S. dollar bills, the inscription, "In God We Trust." In my opinion, if there can be any description of God, it would have to include "changelessness." God is perfection and therefore changeless. If God had to change or if God *could* change, God's perfection would immediately be negated, for perfection needs no change. We "trust," which is synonymous with the word "know," that which we see as *stable* or changeless. We can trust God because by nature God can be trusted. Why? because God is *always* there, and will not–and *cannot*–change. The perfect relationship that we share will always be there.

Love of Self Will Keep You Consistent

Let's keep this simple. If you care about yourself and if you appreciate what God has given you in body, mind, and spirit, you will honor His gifts by taking care of what you have. Unlike narcissistic self-indulgence based on insecurity of not being or having enough, self-love is based on an appreciation and gratitude for who you are, and what you have. We recognize that it is our responsibility to preserve and honor what has been given to us. If you need a reason to get up and go to the gym in the morning, know that it is a blessing to be able to get out of bed. (There has got to be someone in a nearby hospital who wishes he or she could have the ability to get up and walk.) If you have decided to save 10% of your income for 5 years in order to invest in real estate to improve the security of your future, you demonstrate that you care about yourself; this self-care will motivate you to remain consistent. If you decide to return to school in order to learn a new career to improve the quality of life, you will remain consistent until you achieve your goal. This is the power love of self to keep you consistent.

Love of Others Will Keep You Consistent

One of the most powerful motivators to keep you consistent is the love of others. I love my daughter. She is the most precious being on the face of this earth. There is nothing that I wouldn't do for her. When it comes to doing anything that requires consistency for the well-being of my daughter, consistency is a piece of cake. The day that I decided to save $1300 per month for 2 years, in order to invest in our future through real estate investment, made remaining consistent a much easier task than if my motivation was based mostly or solely on self. When you love someone, temporary pain, discomfort, or sacrifice becomes worth bearing because of your willingness to do whatever it takes. I believe that life's greatest experience is love, and as my daughter once said when she was only 14-years-old, "You've got to go through equal suffering for equal greatness." For the love of others, consistency becomes worth the price to pay.

Love of "God" Will Keep You Consistent

Love of God, however you define the Ultimate Organizing Intelligence of the universe, will keep you consistent to the degree of your faith and devotion. God is your Ultimate Accountability Partner. It is not Santa Claus but the Almighty "who knows when you are sleeping and knows when you are wake, who knows when you are good or bad, so be *consistent* for goodness sake."

It has been said that who you are is God's gift to you, and who you become is your gift to God. With that said, anything that you commit to doing for the betterment of yourself and the betterment of others is your gift to God. Striving to do and be your best, remaining steadfast when challenges and opposition arise, and continuing to courageously move forward in spite of it all, is a way of loving God. Love of God will keep you consistent.

You Know a Person By Their Consistency

My dear mother, may she rest in peace, had a saying, "I can't hear what you're saying because I'm too busy watching what you're doing." The message here is that it doesn't matter what a person *says*, what he or she *will* do, it only matters what a person *does* or is actually doing. It is by the fruit that we know the tree; it is not by the fruit that the tree *brags* about producing some day in a distant future.

People who are unpredictable and moody, changing from one day to the next are those with whom establishing a stable relationship becomes next to impossible. To know is to trust, and to trust is to know. These are interchangeable concepts. It is only with the person who is consistent with his or her behavior that we can truly say we know them and trust them.

Consistency of Right Action is Love Expressed

There are many ways to measure the presence of love in a relationship, but consistent right action is the most accurate. The words "I love you" are only validated by what I do. In the deepest sense, I don't think that relationships exist to make us "happy," I feel that relationships exist to afford the opportunity to give of ourselves to another. The happiness of you and the other becomes an inevitable byproduct when giving becomes the primary goal. Understanding, patience, honesty, loyalty, and forgiving result with right action, and right action results in the experience of true love.

Consistent Kindness Outweighs Sincere Apologies

I had a "friend" once, by the name of David, who was very involved with Alcoholics Anonymous because of his addiction to alcohol. He had done very well to stay sober for a long period of time, and later he became a sponsor for new members who needed guidance on the principals and precepts of the group. I remember that one of the principals that he always mentioned to me was the principal of making amends to all those whom you may have harmed in the past because of the alcoholism. He explained the importance of contacting the person who was harmed, showing remorse, recognizing the harm that was done, asking for forgiveness, and being willing to accept whatever the response was given from the person supposedly offended.

Later I noticed a very peculiar behavior pattern of David. On many ocassions, he could be rude and verbally offensive to me with very little provocation. There was one day that he invited me to this Hindu-style temple to meditate. I declined, and said that I was not up to doing it. Upon my refusal, he became enraged, and told me to get out of his house. I left. Three days later, he calls me. "Charles, it was very rude of me to kick you out of my house. I was wrong to do that. You didn't deserve that. I am asking your forgiveness, and I can understand however it is that you may feel." His apology felt so sincere that I said, "Don't worry about it, David, anybody can have a bad moment." A couple of weeks pass, and we are out one evening talking at a coffee shop. I say, "Well, David, it's 8:00 p.m. I need to get home. I will see you later." "What do you mean, 'I will see you later'?" he responds, "You have to give me a ride home!" "I *have* to give you a ride home!" I retort. "If you are going to let me take the bus, forget you and you f...-ing friendship!" "That's fine with me," I replied. I got up and left. I turned around and saw him sitting in the café angry, frowning, and fuming. Two days later, I get a phone call. "Hello, Charles, this is David. It was very rude of me to demand that you give me a ride to my house. I was wrong to do that. You didn't deserve that. I am asking your forgiveness, and I can understand however it is that you may feel." I then hung up the phone without saying a word.

David was the only person whom I had ever met who was a "professional apologizer." He liberally allowed himself emotional outbursts because he *enjoyed* the feeling of the faux-humility he gave himself from apologizing, while asking for the other person's forgiveness.

Consistency Creates Expectancy

Give your wife a flower every Friday for 6 months, and she will expect it. Rub your pet dog on the stomach every day when you come home, and in 3 months, and he will expect it. Give your daughter $50 every week, and soon, she will expect it.

"Consistently Improving" is Relationship Success

All relationships have their ups-and-downs. There will be good days and "bad" days, but the important thing is that we have days. As long as a relationship is consistently improving and consistently growing, we can say that the relationship is a success.

"You've got to go through equal suffering for equal greatness." – Luzemily Prosper *(at 14-years-old)*

Commitment and Consistency

Unbeknownst to most people, the so-called handicapped ironically have an unfair advantage over "normal" people when it comes to having intense commitment and consistency within themselves. (I use the term *normal* tongue-in-cheek because normalcy cannot be measured by such an artificial criterion as physical disability.) Even the term *handicapped* is a judgement call for the assumption is made that, because of some physical disadvantage, the so-handicapped individual is unable to do what other so-called normal people can. I have found in many extraordinary cases that just the opposite of this perception is true. Unusual physically-challenged individuals can develop such strong character and determination that they are able to do things which far surpass those who are born without any physical limitations. This phenomena can also be seen in the case of the economically disadvantaged, individuals who are born in abject poverty, yet move on to become among the wealthiest of modern society. How is this possible? Why is this? In a word: commitment. The commitment of the initially disadvanged can become far greater than those of us who take for granted what we have. The greater the commitment, the greater the consistency. People of greater commitment, just don't give up. They keep going, and inevitably they succeed when others fail, that is, when others give up.

The so-called disadvantaged and handicapped, who go on to do outstanding things, that make us look on in awe, can do so because these individuals develop a strong sense of purpose which keeps them motivated. They become the "chosen ones" to be an inspiration to others who would believe that there are things that they cannot do. The so-called disadvantaged, who go on to achieve great things, are inspired by a sense of gratefulness for the chance to show the world the possibilities of human achievement *in spite of* any perceived disadvantages or disability. This motivation and fire to show the world who *they* have chosen to be is far greater than any of the "ordinary" challenges and setbacks that most people face toward fulfilling their goals. Facing and overcoming obstacles is what the disadvantaged do best.

It's interesting, just as I was changing the font style for some of the letters this page, I noticed these choices:
- Regular
- *Italic*
- **Bold**
- ***Bold Italic.***

I found it interesting that they didn't choose to call Regular "Normal" nor was *Italic* called *"Disadvantaged."* Maybe there is a message here to show us how we might view the differences of each other.

Nick Vujicic (No Arms, No Legs, No Worries!)

One of the most amazing individuals I have ever come across is Nick Vujicic. Nick Vujicic, born December 4, 1982 is, at present, a 32-year-old Christian evangelist and motivational speaker, who was born with a tetra-amelia. Tetra-amelia is a very rare disease where the individual is born literally without any arms or legs. There are only vestiges of feet, which allow the person to walk by moving carefully from side to side.

What is amazing about this young man is that through his faith in God and his commitment to be a miracle for others, he has achieved and continues to achieve far more than most of us who have all of our limbs. As can be expected, Nick grew up confused and in despair as a child, not understanding how "God" could impose such an infliction on him, but as Nick shares in his book, *Unstoppable, The Incredible Power of Faith in Action,* published 2012 by Random House in the Introduction on page 3:

> I was wrong on all counts. I was not alone in my suffering. In fact, many people have dealt with challenges that surpass mine. And God not only loves me, he created me for purposes that I never could have envisioned as a child. He uses me in ways that continue to surprise and amaze me each and every day.

Nick not only finished college, he has a double bachelor's degree in both accounting and financial planning. At the age of seventeen, he started his own non-profit organization, *Life Without Limbs.* Nick has spoken to crowds of as large as 110,000 people. Nick enjoys skydiving, skateboarding, and, yes, even soccer! On the cover of his book *Unstoppable,* there is a picture of him with his charismatically recognizable smile, surfboarding on waves as they splash to his sides. On February 12, 2012, Nick married "drop-dead gorgeous" Kanae Miyahara, whom he describes in his book as truly the greatest gift he has ever received, after his salvation and relationship with Jesus. Nick, a longtime resident of Australia, now lives in Southern California with his wife and their first child. Nick has become one of the most eloquent messengers that faith, a sense of purpose, a commitment to something greater than yourself can make you unstoppable.

The Most Committed Body Builder I've Ever Seen

The other morning at the gym, I was doing leg raises on the abdominal board when a tall and nicely built gentleman, who looked in his mid to late thirties, walked in front of me. He was carefully moving toward the Nautilus fitness machines. He touched the top of one of the machines designed to excercise the shoulder muscles, sat down, and vigorously began to workout. When he finished, he reached to the side and grabbed a thin white cane with a red tip that was resting on a pillar near his equipment. When he got up, I realized, as he turned to walk to next machine, that he was blind. I watched as he gracefully moved from one piece of equipment to another, exercising his various body parts, while intermittently going to the fountain on the far wall for a sip of water. This is commitment with no excuses, and when I am there at 5:30 a.m., I will see my sightless bodybuilding colleague consistently taking care of business.

Helen Keller Was Committed and Consistent

One of the most famous and inspirational figures of the 20th century was Helen Keller, born June 27, 1880. At 19 months of age as a baby, Ms. Keller contracted an illness that was described by doctors at the time as "an acute congestion of the stomach and the brain" which might have been diagnosed as meningitis or scarlet fever today. This illness left her both deaf and blind. Nevertheless, Helen Keller became the first deafblind person to earn a bachelor of arts degree and went on to become a world-famous speaker and author, who wrote over 12 books advocating for women's rights and people with disabilities. However, much of the accomplishments of Helen Keller may not have happened without the commitment and dedication of her teacher, Anne Sullivan, who showed Keller how to transcend her so-called disability and discover talents and abilities that were only waiting to be developed and blossom forth. Helen Keller was committed and consistent, and Anne Sullivan was the quintessential example of teacher/accountability partner.

Why Foreigners Become More Successful Than Americans

First of all, I'm not saying that *all* foreigners become more successful than *all* Americans. I am asking why do *some* foreigners become more successful that <u>most</u> Americans? Yes, let's be honest, you see it all of the time, and you can find it in any major city in the U.S. When opportunity has been limited in their country of origin, and a person dreams of a better life, all the while promising him or herself, that if given chance, he or she will make a success of themselves; there wells within them an incredible fire of determination. The mindset of this type of individual is one of commitment and unstoppable consistency until their goal has been reached.

I don't need to go far from home to give an example of this. Back in 1986, when I first opened my balloon and party store, I hired Winston Merchan, a young man from Ecuador about the age of 22, who spoke no English and had no connections other than his sister, Elvis, whom I had met through a mutual friend. Elvis asked if I could give him a job working as a party balloon decorator for me on the weekends. Since he looked like an eager and honest individual, I said, sure, and Winston worked for me for about a year. During this time, Winston shared with me his dream of opening his own dental lab, working as the professional who creates the replacement teeth and implants ordered by dentists.

Thinking I was saving him much unneeded frustration and disappointment, *in all of my infinite wisdom*, I told him that it would be very difficult to start a business, such as that one here in the United States with no connections, no money, and not being able to speak the language. A year after he worked for me, Winston landed a job as an assistant in a dental lab, since he had had a training and experience doing this job back in his country. I lost track of Winston for about 26 years.

One evening in 2013, I am sitting in an open air café area having a cheese crepe with my daughter, Luzemily, right after watching a movie. Linda Pulido, who also worked for me in my store at the same time I had hired Winston walked up to me and in Spanish said to me with a smile, "¿Te acuerdas de mí?" which is, "Do you remember me?" Since Linda was 20-years-old at the time, and her 47-year-old face that now wore glasses, threw me off for a moment. When I looked to the side, I saw Winston standing next to her. Winston was easy to recognize, as giant standing 5 feet tall, and in spite of being a 49-year-old friend and former employee, I knew who he was. We joyfully gave each other an embrace, and they explained that they had got married after Winston left working for me, and they introduced us to Ashley, their 13-year-old daughter.

"I'd like to invite you and Luzemily to spend a weekend at our home in Simi Valley," said Winston. (Hint: Simi Valley is one of the most upscale areas in Southern California.) "I'd like to show you my dental lab, which is only a couple miles from where we live."

On the day that my daughter and I arrive, we are blown away by the gorgeous, palatial estate that Winston and Linda had achieved. Swimming pool, poolside grill with barbecue area, 4 bedrooms, two floors, and a living room fit for a king. Winston explained that this was the *second* house that he had purchased and that the first one, he is renting out to a tenant. His present home is worth well over a million and he has at least $500,000 equity already built in it. He is expected to pay it out in a few more years. When we go to his dental lab, we see the most modern equipment imaginable. Some of his machines that scan the exact size and position of teeth are worth over $100,000 a piece. Also, I might mention that he has completely paid for the building which houses his lab and owns it free and clear. His clients are among the rich and famous of Simi Valley, and by the way, I must add that he mastered

English and participates in many high-powered dental association meetings. I don't know Winston's exact net worth, but piecing together all of the things that I have seen and heard, I would definitely say that he is worth well over a million dollars.

Now, where would Winston have been if he had listened to *me* 27 years ago trying to tell him how near next to impossible it was going to be to start a dental lab in the United States with no money, no English, and no connections? That goes to show you, even well-intentioned but mis-informed friends and associates will misguide you every time when their message is that you can't, or that it's going to be too difficult. I am so glad that he just ignored me, went ahead, and became successful anyway.

Winston has already done for me a permanent bridge and dental implant replacements. He does excellent work. So, if you are having any dental implants or replacement teeth done in the Southern California area or in any other area, for that matter, I highly recommend that you have your dentist contact:

WM Dental Studio
1975 Royal Ave., Suite 2
Simi Valley, California 93065
(805) 584-5030

The Mother Who *Had* to Become a Millionaire

It was a long time ago that I read the story about a mother who worked as a maintenance worker for a local university. Her job was simple and consisted of cleaning the classrooms, library, and the restrooms in the afternoon and the evening after the students had gone home for the day. Her income was enough to take care of herself and her 15-year-old daughter who lived with her. All was well until her daughter was diagnosed with a rare illness causing slow deterioration of her body that would require frequent and expensive treatments that her job's insurance plan could not cover. She thought, "My God, the only way that I could ever afford those treatments would be to become a millionaire!" Right there, she got her answer, and somehow she made the decision to make it happen. This lady, as I remember in the story, got a friend to introduce her to a realtor who committed himself to helping her learn how to invest in real estate. This realtor loaned this mother the down payment for her first home purchase, and showed her how to buy the next property and the next based on the equity of the first and then each preceding property. This mother eagerly and consistently did what she was instructed to do. When she had a problem with a tenant or with property maintenance, she solved it. When she had any delays in getting her next loan, she found a way to make it happen. Her motivation was always in finding a way to finance her daughter's medical treatments, which had then become possible after the purchase of the first 2 properties. Within 5 years, this mother not only had found a way to pay for her daughter's medical treatment, she had accumulated a net worth in real estate of over one million dollars.

Know *Why* You Must Remain Committed

If commitment and consistency are two sides of the same coin, the question then becomes why you must remain committed. The importance of the *why*, will keep you consistent. The importance of your commitment is your buffer against the problems and challenges that you must meet along the way. You can say to yourself, "I know this won't be easy, but I know it will be worth it." A sense of purpose as expressed through love of self and love of others, keeps you going strong while people who have not discovered a greater purpose for what must be done will usually quit at the first sign of opposition.

The *why* will determine the likelihood of your success.

Quitting is Never and Option

Quitting and remaining consistent are mutually exclusive. You must choose either the path well-trodden by most or the path less traveled. Robert Frost, put it this way in his classic poem:

The Road Not Taken

Two roads diverged in a yellow wood,
And sorry I could not travel both
And be one traveler, long I stood
And looked down one as far as I could
To where it bent in the undergrowth;

Then took the other, as just as fair,
And having perhaps the better claim
Because it was grassy and wanted wear,
Though as for that the passing there
Had worn them really about the same,

And both that morning equally lay
In leaves no step had trodden black.
Oh, I kept the first for another day!
Yet knowing how way leads on to way
I doubted if I should ever come back.

I shall be telling this with a sigh
Somewhere ages and ages hence:
Two roads diverged in a wood, and I,
I took the one less traveled by,
And that has made all the difference.

"Consistency is far better than rare moments of greatness." – Anonymous

Sudden Deviation from Routine Threatens Consistency

We have already established that same-time same-place routine reinforces consistency; the opposite of this is also true. When we suddenly shift or change an established routine, this will disrupt continuity, and consistency will be compromised. If you have achieved consistency in any activity through organization and discipline over time, it is because your psycho-biological organism is now on autopilot. Upon starting, you quickly "get into the groove" and continue with your daily routine with minimal effort.

Let us say that you are in college and that you have established a firm routine of studying for 2 hours between 3:00 and 5:00 p.m. This has been a solid practice for more than 3 months. Studying one day at 3:00 p.m. for two hours, and then the next day, attempting to study for one hour at noon and for another hour at 6:00 p.m., will definitely compromise your previously established pattern. The universe likes order and repeatable rhythms. Changing, for example, from one study schedule to another may work for a while, but it will never equal the power, elegance, and efficiency of a consistent daily routine.

When the Unexpected Interrupts Your Routine

The most tenous time to allow interruptions in routine is in the beginning. In the first few weeks, before an established automatic mindset becomes apparent, it is advisable to avoid deviating from your same-time, same-place program. One acquaintance told me with excitement how he was on a roll for the first two weeks, going to bed early and getting up early the next morning to exercise. Then he was invited to a party one Friday night, which kept him up until 1:00 a.m. When he got home, he told me he slept until pass 9:30 a.m. the next day. He explained that since he "didn't *feel* like" exercising on *that* day that he would make it up the *next* day. The problem with this type of thinking is that you can never "make up" for a missed day – because it is *not the same day.* To make a long story short, the next time I saw him was two months later, I asked how his exercise program was going. The response was, "Well, I got off my game a few times, and I realize I have to get back into it again. Just can't find the time right now."

Rituals Reinforce Consistency

Whether we realize it or not all of us have rituals of activity that are carried out every day of our lives. The irony is that some of our daily rituals lead us closer to what we say we want out of life, while other rituals move us farther away. For some, their daily or evening ritual may be to get home from work, plop a frozen dinner into the oven, grab a beer, turn on the cable channels, and spend several hours watching the featured movie of the week. Get to bed by 11:00 p.m. and fall asleep by 11:15 p.m. Hear the alarm ring at 7:00 a.m. Lie in bed until the last minute, then get up and rush to work. Once at work, spend the rest of the day wishing it was time to go home. This is a gross exaggeration of a ritual that consistently moves in a direction of non-achievement and a life without purpose.

For others, daily rituals are carefully planned, which lead to steady and consistent movement toward a worthwhile goal. A positive daily ritual might be, to get home early after work, eat a healthy well-prepared meal, study real estate investment strategies for an hour, meditate, lay out the clothes for the next morning, and go to bed by 8:30 p.m. Get up by 4:30 a.m. Eat and be to the gym by 5:30 a.m. Exercise for 45 minutes, shower, dress, and be to work at least 30 minutes early. Spend the rest of day being grateful for employment and opportunity and being able to save and invest in the future.

All rituals are conscious choices in the beginning and they take some time getting used to, but eventually rituals take on a life of their own and begin to work for you without having to think about them. It becomes an automatic and natural part of your day. Which direction your ritual takes you depends on your goals (or lack of them). Life always flows. There is no standing still. You can move forward by choice or slide backward by default. Choose wisely.

Record-Keeping Aides Consistency

Motivation keeps moving you forward as you get closer an closer to your goal. So, what fuels motivation? Achievement reinforces motivation, but achievement must be made evident. Achievement is made evident through measurement, and measurement leads to greater achievement through record-keeping. How can we know that progress has even taken place unless there is some way that we can see it? Progress is essentially a comparison of where we were to where we are now. Thus when progress is measured, we call this proof. Results don't lie, and results are why we are working so diligently. Why keep going if there no evidence that we are moving forward? Record-keeping will allow us to see the degree and extent of how we are doing. Record-keeping does not have to be extensive nor complicated. How record-keeping is done can depend a lot on the task and type of goal that is sought. For example, if you are running a business, record-keeping might take the form of having an accountant show you profit-and-loss statements on a monthly basis. If you are working toward losing 10 lbs. of bodyfat, you might weigh yourself in the beginning and then periodically weigh yourself once or twice a week and then record the results of that day on a wall calendar. Generally speaking, record-keeping can be as simple and generic as keeping a detailed written diary in which you make an entry of a paragraph to say how things are going. Record-keeping not only tells you how your are progressing, it also points you to the areas that might need improvement. Because plans are meant to be flexible and pliable, with the right information and feedback, you can tweek what you have been doing, make any needed adjustments or changes. Taking this approach, a "setback" becomes *feedback*, which allows you to make the needed corrections to continue moving forward.

One Drop of Water Won't Change a Tea's Color

In a book that I read many years ago, *Aikido in Daily Life* by Koichi Tohei, first published in 1966 by Rikugei Pubishing House, the author gave what I thought was the perfect metaphor of how change, persistence, and consistency take place. On page 124, Tohei explains the process of how bad habits are changed to good habits by giving oneself the correct subconscious suggestions, over time. He writes:

> One drop of clear water added to a cup of tea will change neither its color nor its taste. Two drops will do little more, but if drop by drop we continue to add water, both the color and the flavor will alter. People generally leap to the conclusion because one or two drops of effort cannot change the subconscious, it is impossible to change it. The truth is that, just as with the cup of tea, if we continue the effort, it will alter.

There is great simplicity and elegance in this explanation.

Immediate Results Cannot Co-Exist with Consistency

The greatest drawback to consistency is impatience. Consistency can only be experienced over time. Time is the co-worker of consistency. Given enough time, you can not only see consistency, but consistency becomes stronger with each repetition. Stages have to be passed and thresholds have to be reached. A body at rests tends to stay at rest until acted upon by an outside force, so says Newton's first law of motion. This is to say that any new habit that is to be formed must overcome the inertia or resistance to move in the opposite direction. In a sense, if you are moving to the left, metaphorically speaking, the movement to the right is at rest. The movement to the right is inert, relative to the movement to the left. There is resistance to move right, and the outside force which changes direction is a combination of decision, determination, and persistence. Once inertia is broken, momentum takes over and consistency becomes easier and easier, providing that you persist. Persistence thus is repeated and regulated daily by choice, doing the same thing over and over, which is designed to move you closer and closer to your ultimate goal.

Give Yourself a 30-Day "Consistency Challenge"

When embarking upon a big-time goal, what has to be done may create a sense of overwhelm. There is a problem by projecting too much into the future in an attempt to visualize the long road ahead. When overwhelm sets in, so does procrastination. And unlike some would mistakenly believe, procrastination has nothing to do with "laziness" or lack of ambition. Procrastination has everything to do with fear, the fear of being unable to carry it out, the fear of it being "too much" to do. If you are a regular reader of motivation style books, you may have heard the answer to this question. Well, here goes. Do you know how to eat an elephant?...Bite, by, bite. My love for packyderms notwithstanding, this cheesy question is meant to illustrate the principle of gradualness. So, we embrace the 30-day Consistency Challenge. I would recommend that when you have made a decision to make a major lifestyle change, which may require some sacrifice and discipline, to *not* attempt to commit totally to the idea all at once. If your major goal may involve a 3-year gestation period, commit to only 30-days of this new change. You can even break this 30-day challenge into 4 separate weeks. Set a goal of just completing the 1st week. Once you complete the first week, commit to completing the second week, and so on and so forth until you reach week 4. If at any time you miss a day in this 30-day trial period, start again, but start again by counting from day 1 of a *new* 30-day trial. This second round should be even easier because you probably have managed to put in a least a few days or a few weeks. The key word is intention, focus, and the willingness to begin again if necessary. With this approach, you will do 30 consecutive days without missing, and you will be well on your way in establishing a new habit and way of life.

Unscheduled Free Time Compromises Consistency

I remember when I was in graduate school, that I accomplished more when I had to plan my time within a strict schedule of multiple assignments to complete, than when I was on 3-week vacation with lots of free time to schedule whenever I wanted and how much I wanted. Too much unstructured time leads to more time wasted, than when there is tight schedule. I believe that the reason for this is because we usually can only appreciate the value of time by comparison. You are more likely to waste time if you assumed that you had the next 10 years to begin an important task than if you *knew* that you only had the next 10 years to live. When you work at a 9:00 to 5:00 that provides you marginal job satisfaction, you are more likely to look forward to and value your two-day weekend. A two-day weekend, after working all week can seem more delicious that paid retirement where you are not obligated to do anything all day. The message is clear: unscheduled free time is anathema, and structured, goal-oriented, and well-planned time is productive, creative, and satisfying.

Seeing Results Reinforces Consistency

We plan, motivate ourselves, and do what is necessary to see results. Results are what feed the fire of persistence. The better you plan, the more you persist, while remaining consistent of course, the more results you will see. Results perpetuate the circle of success for again you will persist, remain consistent, and then see even more results.

"Great things require consistency." –
Anonymous

Consistency Is How the Universe Works

How is it that we can go out every day of the year and never have to worry about the sky falling? Though silly and frivolous on the surface, the answer to this question reveals a profound and awesome reality of how the universe works. We can go out confidently without the worry that the sky will fall, that gravity will stop working, or that the sun will suddenly go dark because we have consistently seen that the opposite to all of this is true. We know that certain scientific laws keep the universe together and operating in a predictable way. *Webster's New World Dictionary,* 2003, page 366, defines **law** as "a sequence of natural events occurring with unvarying uniformity under the same conditions." Though flawed, this is a pretty good initial attempt to define a "law." I say flawed because neither "unvarying uniformity" nor "same conditions" can ever be proven any more than a "straight" line; these are theoretical constructs, which attempt to conceptualize that which is unmeasureable. Notwithstanding, this is a good beginning to understanding that the universe operates within a structure of reliable principles we call laws. Scientific laws are based on consistency, and scientific laws are established because of their consistent cause and effect relationship. "What goes up, must come down" has been the consistent law of gravity since the beginning of time. We "know" a law by its reliable, consistent, and "unchangeable" nature. And it is even interesting how we say that we *know* something. Examined very closely, *knowing* is no more that *believing* something without doubt. With enough consistent observation, over time, there is a point that we declare *knowledge* of that which is observed. However, underlying the assertion of all knowledge is a strong *belief* in the reliable, consistent, and unchangeable nature of what we observe or conceive to be true.

Belief = trust, and trust = a feeling of security. A feeling of security = peace of mind. Peace of mind is the ultimate goal of all human existence whether, individually, we realize this or not. Pleasure is a poor subsitute for peace of mind because **pleasure** is <u>unreliable</u> *(it is here today - gone tomorrow)*, <u>inconsistent</u> *(it may bring happiness now, but may not be there tomorrow)*, and is <u>changeable</u> *(what was pleasureable 10 years ago may no longer serve you today.)*

So, are "happiness" and peace of mind the same? Happiness is a type of pleasure, which has an opposite called "sadness." Peace of mind has no opposite and can *co-exist* during moments of either happiness or sadness. So, to conclude, even though we may not consciously feel "happy" that gravity works when we go outside for a walk, we do feel *peace of mind* to go outside without the worry that we will float up endlessly into space.

Cycles Are the Core of Universal Consistency

It takes just a little observation to notice that cycles pervade all areas and all aspects of life. It is how the universe can manage a mind-boggling multiplicity of events simultaneous occurring without one activity seriously impacting or impeding the other. There are large cycles and small cycles. There are cycles within cycles. Some cycles may last a few seconds while other cycles may repeat themselves every year, every hundred years, or more.

The first thing that you notice about a cycle is that it consistently repeats itself in a similarly uniform way in that, if studied, can be predicted with reasonable accuracy. Approximately every 12 hours of the day, there will be a sunrise followed by a sunset approximately 12 hours later. In order for traffic to flow easily through intersections, there is a cycle of red light, yellow light, and green light. You generally get up to work at a certain hour, which is followed by a typical hour that you go home. We normally go to bed at a certain time and wake at a certain time. While we are asleep, there is a dream cycle; approximately every 90 minutes, we dream, whether we remember the dream upon awakening or not. Curly hair happens because it grows in a cycle of spurts; it grows, then pauses; it grows, then pauses; this start-stop growth is what creates the curl. A woman has her period, barring abnormalities, every 28 days. Should the woman become pregnant, the average gestation period preceding birth happens every 9 months. Breathing is cyclic. Adults normally take 12 to 20 breaths per minute. Strenuous exercise drives the breath rate up to an average of 45 breaths per minute. Some people blink about 6 blinks per minute, while others may blink as much a 30 blinks per minute. Eye blink rates can vary from person to person, but what is for sure is that each person has a measurable average-blink-rate. In fact, a blink rate could not exist were it not measureable and cyclic. If we step back just a bit, we can remind ourselves of the grand life cycle to which we are all subjected: conception, birth, growth, aging, and death.

Consistent Growth Defines Survival

Growth and consistency become equivalent to survival. I can say that this relates to physical survival, emotional survival, and spiritual survival.

A human cell must consistently grow to survive. Once a sperm fertilizes the ovum, that *zygote* (the fertilized sperm and egg) must immediately begin to consistently divide and grow in order to survive. Cessation of growth means certain death.

That cessation of growth means certain death is no less true on an emotional level as well. As we pass from infant to toddler, to adolescent, to adult, there must be a consistent emotional growth, or what we call maturity, in order for the adult to survive in the real world. Emotional maturity is a survival mechanism. A person with little or no emotional maturity is not likely to have the discipline to survive and thrive. An emotionally immature person shuns both discipline and responsibility. They procrastinate a lot. They blame others rather than seeing themselves as first cause. Denial is the mechanism by which all pseudo-solutions become possible. Pseudo-solutions are usually excesses of some sort which divert and distract the mind from facing whatever happens to be the real cause of the problem. Pseudo-solutions can take the form of anything in excess, which can be sex, drugs, food, music, or any other "normal" diversion taken to the extremes.

A person who does not consistently grow spiritually will, generally speaking, only have rare moments of inner peace and a sense of purpose. Gratitude becomes foreign, and people, events, and material things never seem "enough;" they never satisfy the "soul."

The Planets *Consistently* Revolve

In the next several sections of this chapter, I would like to show how consistency plays an integral part of how the universe must operate. All that we can see, feel, touch, and all that we can't see, feel, and touch is governed by law and order. Law and order by definition must operate consistently. If "what goes up and must come down" operates today, but maybe not tomorrow, but again for the next three days afterwards, and then does not happen for the next two years would hardly be seen as law and order. If the planets did not follow a consistent cyclic pattern of revolving around each other, they would have collided a long time ago. But planets, solar systems, and galaxies have been revolving around each other for eons of time. Without a consistent and ordered pattern of revolution, none of this miracle would have ever been possible.

The Seasons *Consistently* Change

Winter, spring, summer, fall – we can rely on this. There are occasionally anomalies to seasonally rhythms, that is, some summer or winter temperatures may start a little later or a little earlier than usual, but the sequential order does not change. When studied closer, I would postulate that even the so-called anomalies happen, when the do happen, in some predictable pattern and cycle. With enough time and careful observation, all cycles can reveal themselves. All movement or activity must exist within its own rhythm and cycle; my reasoning for this is that since there are a myriad of other movements of activities that must co-exist, co-existence is only possible if "everyone drives in their own lane" to use the parlance of freeway traffic control.

The Sun *Consistently* Shines

The sun consistently shines, whether our side of the earth is facing it or not. Another interesting thing about how the sun shines is that the heat does not move in a straight line, it moves in what scientists call *solar waves*. A solar wave is another way of saying that the heat pulsates rhythmically or cyclicly from the sun's surface and outward towards its planets. We are beginning to see that consistent action must repeat itself, and to remain consistent all activity must establish for itself a rhythm of repeatability. This is why carrying out a planned activity that is part of a new goal is best achieved when the planned activity is structured within a *same-time same-place* rhythmic cycle.

Our Heart *Consistently* Beats

The regularity of our heartbeat quintessentially defines consistency. The rhythm of the heartbeat is measured in beats per minute or (bpm). The "average" adult has a resting heart rate of about 60 to 100 beats per minute. As you exercise and become fitter, your resting heart rates may drop from 40 to 60 beats per minute or even lower. I remember having read some where that during deep meditation, your heart beat can go to as low as 10 to 20 beats per minute. (My own experience with meditation corroborates this.)

In this section, we are looking at the incredible consistency of how the heart beats. Let us say that the average heartbeat is about 80 beats per minute. This means that your heart beats about 4,800 times per hour. This is a whopping 115,200 times per day. Over the course of a year, your heart would beat 42,048,000! That is forty-two *million* and 48 thousand times per year! I think that we should stop right now and send some love and gratitude to our amazing heart for the non-stop, relentless job that it carries out to keep us alive. Let's take an even broader look. If you live to 80 years old your precious heart will have beaten approximately 3,363,840,000 times!! That's 3 **billion**, three hundred and sixty-three **million**, and eight hundred and forty thousand times! Your heart is really, really serious about keeping you alive!

Without Consistency, the Universe Ceases to Exist

We mentioned just a few of the many universal phenomena in this chapter: the planets consistenly revolve, the seasons consistenly change, the sun consistenly shines, and our heart consistenly beats. Even with this very small list, the absence of consistency would spell chaos, death, and disaster. Consistency allows all that is to continue to exist.

God is the Original Rhythm of Universal Consistency

In "God," we trust because God is consistent and unchangeable. In "Consistency," we trust because trust is predicated on the existence of consistency. Looking at it this way, consistency is a god-like quality, which, when directed toward a worthwhile goal leads us to self-fulfillment and self-realization.

"Long-term consistency trumps short-term intensity." – *Bruce Lee*

10

Consistency Will Trump Talent Every Time

So far we have established that success is a gold coin with consistency on one side and persistence on the other. I would like to start this chapter with one of my favorite quotes from Calvin Coolidge, the 30th president of the United States:

> Nothing in this world can take the place of persistence. Talent will not: nothing is more common than unsuccessful men with talent. Genius will not; unrewarded genius is almost a proverb. Education will not: the world is full of educated derelicts. Persistence and determination alone are omnipotent.

This is Prosper's version of President Coolidge's quote:

> **Nothing** in this world can take the place of *persistence* and *consistency*. **Talent** will not: nothing is more common than unsuccessful men with talent. **Genius** will not; unrewarded genius is almost a proverb. **Education** will not: the world is full of educated derelicts. *Persistence* and *consistency* alone are omnipotent.

Would You Rather Be Very Talented or Very Consistent?

Talent is the potential to do, while consistency is the action of doing. The universe rewards action. The universe does not reward *potential* action. Unless talent is utilized and utilized consistently, it is like a bicycle that sits in the corner of a room that is never taken out for a spin. Genius is only *interesting* when small glimpses are seen and not used to change lives and make the world a better place. Higher education and advanced degrees are no guarantee of success. In fact education, for some, can become a barrier to successfully taking action.

I remember an acquaintance a long time ago who told me that she wanted to start her own business. At the time, she had graduated from high school and was making her choice of college. She told me that since she was interested in her own business that it probably would be best to major in business administration in college. I mentioned that even though this major would be helpful, if she truly wanted to start her own business, she could start acting on that immediately and learn as she'd go along. She got her B.S. in Business Administration in four years, yet still had not taken steps toward starting any business idea. "I think that to really become successful, I need to get my Masters in Business Administration," she replied.

Two years later, she had an MBA. "Now what?" I asked. "Well, if I study for my doctorate, I could teach on the university level and with all of that knowledge and information, I could maybe start my business and ..."

In the case of this lady, "getting more education" allowed her to mask her fear of starting and taking the leap of faith. As long as she could convince herself that she didn't have "enough" education, she could believe that she was not ready to start. She was stuck in a perpetual state of "getting ready" rather than getting started.

In the next section, I would like to use a classic Aesop's Fable children's tale to illustrate the power of persistence.

The Tortoise and the Hare

There was once an incredibly speedy hare who always bragged about how fast he could run to a tortoise called Slow and Steady. Slow and Steady, became tired of hearing him boast, so, he challenged him to a race. All the animals laughed at the idea of the tortoise challenging the hare. Then arrived the day and they all gathered in the forest to watch.

Hare ran down the road with lightning-like speed from the opening shot of the gun, then, after a short while, he paused on the side of a tree to rest. He turned around and looked back at Slow and Steady, who was still far behind, and laughed out, "How do you expect to beat me in this race when you are walking along at such a slow, slow pace?"

Hare stretched himself out against a tree and decided to take a nap. He thought, "There is plenty of time to rest and relax."

Slow and Steady walked and walked. Relentlessly he pressed on step-by-step. While Hare was sleeping, Slow and Steady continued – until he could see the finish line! Slow and Steady continued. He never, ever stopped. Finally, he came to the finish line!

The cheers of the animals were so loud that the noise and excitement suddenly woke Hare up.

Startled and realizing that Tortoise was winning the race, Hare made a last minute dash to catch up to win. But it was too late. Tortoise was already over the finish line. Slow and Steady had won the race!

Consistency trumps talent every time.

Simple Things Consistently Done Surpasses Talent Alone

Innate talent or ability, on the surface, might appear to be the guaranteed advantage for success, but as we saw in the Aesop fable of the tortoise and the hare, the continuous one-step-after-the-other progression is a far superior strategy.

If I could take a fire hose and point 150 pounds per square inch of water pressure against a mountain side for 3 hours, or for an entire day, very little *perceptible* distance would be noticed. However, if tiny drops from a water source were to fall on this same mountain, day after day, week after week, month after month, year after year, decade after decade, century after century – eventually that mountain side would crack and then split in two. Consistency, with enough time, and patience are the only requirements. It matters little how simple the action may be. What matters more is how consistently the simple action is done.

The Daffodil Principle

High in the mountains of San Bernardino in Southern California, you can find an amazing garden the size of five football fields placed side by side containing a golden yellow blanket of over 50,000 daffodils as far as the eye can see. The Daffodil Garden was started back in 1958 by Mrs. Gene Bauer, a retired school teacher and artist who desired to create this garden in the massive open area surrounding her home. When you walk into this area your breath is taken away by its dazzling beauty, you are then given the answers to the immediate questions that are likely to be inside your head. In the midst of all this colorful glory, you will find a well-kept A-frame house, where on the patio, there is a poster with a headline: "Answers to the Questions I Know You Are Asking." The first answer is "50,000 bulbs." The second answer is "One at a time, by one woman. Two hands, two feet, and very little brains." The third answer is "Began in 1958." This has been coined as The Daffodil Principle. Simply put,

The Daffodil Principle is learning how to move toward our goals one step at a time, sometimes by moving just one *baby*-step at a time, and while so doing, learn how to *love* the doing, and discover the magic of time-accumulation which reveals itself through patience. When we accumulate tiny pieces of time, in small increments of daily effort, we discover that we can accomplish extra-ordinary things through very ordinary efforts.

Consistency Is Not for Cowards

What makes people continue to press on in the face of oppostion and setback? Courage. What makes a person persist in the in spite of all challenges? Courage. What therefore must be the driving dynamic behind the forward movement of consistency? Yes, courage. We can say that consistency is not for the weak or "faint of heart." And I literally mean it when I say that consistency is not for the faint of heart. *Webster's New World Dictionary*, 2003, page 152, defines courage: "**courage** (kur´ij) *n.* [[< L. *cor*, heart]] the quality of being brave; valor." I would like you to focus on the etymology of this word. The "cour" of the word *cour*age comes from the Latin root "cor," which means heart. I digress a bit, but the ancient Egyptians, when it was time to mummify their Pharoahs and other important deceased, believed that the seat of the soul was in the *heart*. They believed that the brain served no purpose other than to perhaps produce snot. They therefore, sucked out the brain tissue by inserting a long tube through the nasal cavity and then extracted and discarded the brain gray matter. I can only imagine that the persistence of the Egyptians to build the pyramids and the elaborate tombs of the Pharoahs came from a commitment, which they felt from the "heart."

Success is not the arena for the the weak-willed, indecisive, and fearful. Not everyone is willing to be courageous, face their fears, and press on in spite of all opposition and distractions. It is not a question of whether everyone will do it? It is a question of will *you* do it?

Consistency Is Not for "Excuse Makers"

We are only as successful as the excuses we refuse to live by. I heard it said once that, in life, you can only have one of two things; you can either have reasons or results – *but you can't have both*. Excuses don't work to move you forward. Excuses only work to make you feel comfortable to stay where you are. Excuses are the blinders that keep you from seeing who and what is responsible for where you are and where you are going. My 16-year-old daughter, Luzemily, told me that she was in a history class in high school, and the teacher was trying to make a case or justification for the poor to remain poor. When this teacher asked my daughter her viewpoint on the so-called poor, she said, "It is true that some people are born into disadvantaged circumstances, which may be beyond their control, however, most people *remain* in their circumstances by the poor *choices* they make thereafter." If you really want to do something, you'll find a way; if you don't you'll find an excuse.

Discipline is at the Core of All Consistency

What do you think of when I utter the word "discipline?" There are at least two very distinct and opposite defintions of the word discipline, which is why most people scream and run for the hills where they hear it. (Just kidding.) However, I would like to show the two ways that discipline can be understood. Again, I refer to *Webster's New World Dictionary,* 2003, page 187 to definitions numbered 2 and 3: **dis-ci-pline #2** "training that develops self-control, efficiency, etc." Now contrast this definition with **dis-ci-pline #3** "strict control to enforce obedience." We can see that discipline, which develops self-control and efficiency, is self-chosen a discipline, which is *imposed* to enforce obedience is not the discipline we are interested in. Discipline with the goal of self-control and efficiency is a choice, and it is a choice which can only be renewed each day by the individual.

Talent Can Only Reveal Itself Through Consistency

No matter how talented or naturally gifted you are, no one will ever be able to discover this unless this talent is revealed through consistent use of it. It is not what you have but what you consistenly use of what you have that makes a difference. You can only change the world through the *consistent* use of your talent.

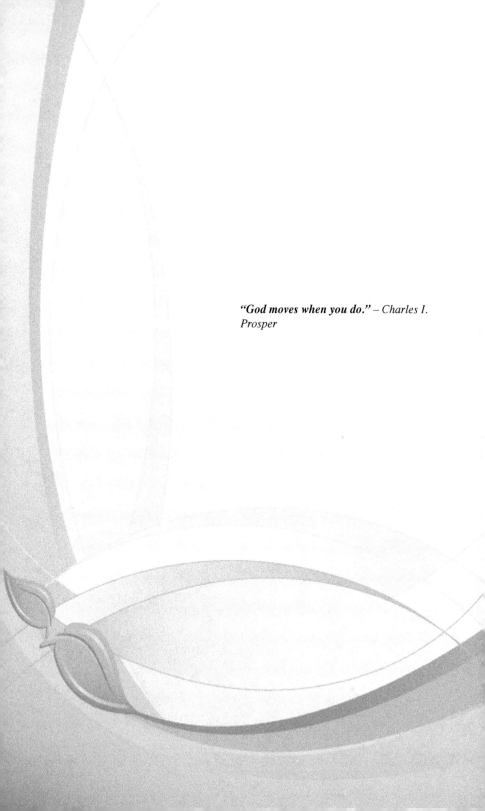

"God moves when you do." – *Charles I. Prosper*

11

How to Become Consistent in 10 Easy Steps

In this chapter, I would like to get basic and very practical. If consistency is the way to success, there must be a way to successful consistency. I have found that there are 10 easy steps to make consistency work for you and become a way of life with those things that are important.

The 10 Steps to Becoming Consistent

Once you understand these steps consciously and put them into action, goal achievement through consistency will become an acquired talent.

1. Set a Goal

There are two ways to set a goal. You can do it in writing, or you can keep it clearly in the forefront of your mind. Either approach will work. The most important thing is that you have specific target, which defines a positive change in circumstances from where you are now to where you intend to be.

2. Create a Plan

Your plan is the body of your consistency. Consistency involves doing certain things in a certain way every day.

This is your plan. Some plans may require that they be written, such as an exercise routine, or a real estate investment strategy, others maybe not.

3. Enlist Accountability Partners

None of us succeed in life alone. We live in a world where we need each other. Your accountability partner will help to keep you on track. An accountability partner could be a coach, counselor, financial advisor, or your spouse, depending on the goal and the situation.

4. Begin Immediately

If something is worth doing, it is worth doing immediately. Success begins once you take action. You cannot take action "tomorrow." You can only *imagine* taking action tomorrow. Action happens in the now.

5. Expect and Overcome Inertia

Consistency doesn't happen by default, and one of the reasons for this is inertia. To begin a plan implies change and a movement in an opposite direction. Procrastination is the dynamic that attempts to keep change from happening until the outside force of your conscious-decision-making moves you in the new direction.

6. Persist (Get Off Track - Get Back On Track)

Rarely is there perfect consistency, especially in the beginning of change. There will be times when you may get off track temporarily; this is normal and to be expected. The first principle of consistency is as soon as you notice you have gotten off track – *get back on track immediately* and continue to move forward.

7. Be Patient – Give It Time

Consistency can only reveal itself through time. Repetition of planned, structured activity leads to the reality of routine. Give yourself a 30-day consistency test, then a next 30-day consistency test, and then a third 30-day consistency test.

8. Do *Something* Each Day – Just Don't Skip

No matter how consistent we are, life happens. There will be some days, where through no fault of our own, they may be interruptions to our complete routine. Interruptions notwithstanding, do something – *anything* – just don't skip.

9. Remind Yourself "Why"

Motivation results from the recognition of an important goal. If the "why" is big enough, the "what" becomes worth doing. Unwittingly, your consistency is predicated on the importance of what you must do. Reminding yourself why becomes the fuel of your persistence.

10. Don't Quit - Ever!

Men don't fail; they only stop trying. Failing only means failing to continue. Winners never quit, and quitters never win. (Hackneyed but true.)

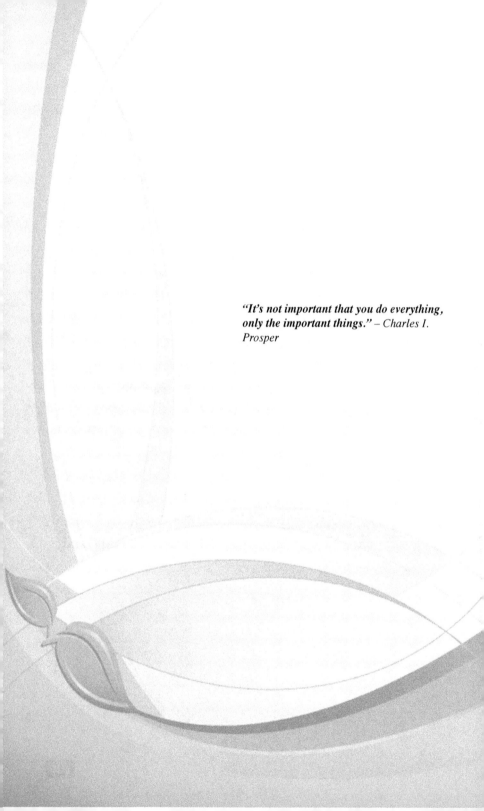

"It's not important that you do everything, only the important things." – *Charles I. Prosper*

12

There Is No Substitute for Consistency

Let us review two key concepts: consistency and persistence. Though they must work together in order for success to happen, they are two distinct dynamics. Consistency is about structured uniformity; you do certain things in a certain way everyday. Consistency is conformity with previous practice. For example, if your goal is a muscular and fit body, generally speaking, you would lift weights and combine it with aerobic activity. This you would do as a routine in a specified way and on specified days. To suddenly change to yoga for a week, then Zumba for the next, then skip for two weeks and start a program of Pilates, is an example of inconsistency.

Persistence, differs from consistency in that it is the *motor* which continues to push you forward. However, much of your success will depend on *how* you move forward. Are you moving forward consistently or inconsistently? If you are following the advice of a financial advisor one week and then change to a different financial advisor the next week, and then to a different one the next week, with each advisor giving you something different and sometimes contradictory advice, persisting with such an *inconsistent* plan will lead you to confusion and failure. When there is constant changing, this leads to confusion, becoming discouraged and then giving up.

However, with a well-thought-out and consistent plan, persistence because your greatest ally to success.

In his timeless book, *Think and Grow Rich* by Napoleon Hill, first published in 1937 and then re-published in 1999 by Wilshire Book Company, Chatsworth, CA, on page 229, there is his classic quote on persistence.

Those who have cultivated the HABIT of persistence seem to enjoy insurance against failure. No matter how many times they are defeated, they finally arrive up toward the top of the ladder. Sometimes it appears that there is a hidden Guide whose duty is to test men through all sorts of discouraging experiences. Those who pick themselves up after defeat and keep on trying, arrive; and the world cries, "Bravo! I knew you could do it!" The hidden Guide lets no one enjoy great achievement without passing the PERSISTENCE TEST. Those who can't take it, simply do not make the grade.

Placing the Perfect Brick

Do not set out to build a wall. Set out to place the perfect brick, and in time, the wall will take care of itself. The practice of consistency comes down to seeing that the one important unit that we call "each day" is all there is and is all that we need. How I will use the present moment is more important that what will happen to me in the future. The fact is, what will happen in the future is predicated on how I use the opportunity of the present-moment-reality by practicing consistency.

Success Formulas Don't Work

If you ever look at the available book titles on the subject of success, you are likely to find a plethora of "step-by-step" success-formulas that are "guaranteed" to lead you to your goals if only you do exactly what the author did.

When it comes to planning the path to your success, you have to look at the unique circumstances of your life. No two persons are surrounded by the exact same circumstances, therefore no set-in-stone success-formula will work for everyone. What I am trying to say is, metaphorically speaking, you will not commit to wearing someone else's shoes when they are not your correct size, when they are either a little too big or a little too small. Create a tailored-made plan for your own unique situation. Create a plan that you will commit to and one to which you will remain consistent.

Consistency Is the Narrow Path to Success

When I say that consistency is the narrow path to success, I mean that, like the road less traveled, you will not find many others like *you* who are willing to do the same. Discipline is difficult, and human nature, left to its own devices, would much prefer "easy." Expect not many people to understand you, and expect even more people to criticize you. What the success-minded individual would call daily-disciplined-activity, the unsuccessful-minded might call obsessive-compulsive behavior. Some times, in fact *most* times, it is better not to even discuss your plans with insignificant others. Silence is strength. Like a steam-driven locomotive, the steam that is contained within, pushes the engine forward. You, like the steam-driven locomotive, through silence, *keep* your power within and *maintain* forward-motion energy instead of "talking it out of your system." In his timeless classic, *The Prophet* by Kahil Gibran, when he speaks of Talking, explains why most people cannot remain silent. He says, "You talk when you cease to be at peace with your thoughts."

I say, choose not to be punctured by the nay-sayers of the world. Act without blowing the trumpet call to the world.

Consistency is a lonely road, and as you scale the pyramid of life from the broad base bottom, where the majority of people choose to stay, and gradually rise to the top, through commitment, consistency, and persistence, you begin to notice, that as the pyramid narrows to the top, where ultimate success is found, it is less crowded, the air is cleaner, and there opens a breathtaking view of all the possibilities of your life.

If Consistency Were Easy, Then Everyone Would Do It

If consistency came natural and without effort, I probably wouldn't have written this book, and you probably wouldn't be reading this section. The fact is that consistency is very counter-intuitive to the human tendency to seek the path of least resistance. If two doors side-by-side lead to the same entrance, the door that is partially opened will usually be the door where most people will enter first. Consistency is not easy, and no one likes difficult, but easy rarely leads to greatness. The greater the struggle, the sweeter the victory. I don't expect everyone to be consistent with the things that they say are important to them, but I can definitely predict *success* for those who choose to do so. Consistency is a choice, and choosing negates losing by default. We *choose* to be successful. We *choose* to be happy. We *choose* to persist until we win.

What Makes *You* Consistent?

We don't procrastinate about everything, no more than we are consistent about everything. We procrastinate with those things that cause us to feel "overwhelmed," and we are consistent with those goals of such importance that cause us to feel, "I will do this no matter what!" Martin Luther King, Jr. once said, "If a man has not discovered something that he will die for, he isn't fit to live." Charles I. Prosper says, "If a man has not discovered something that he will be consistent for, he isn't fit to be successful." So, what are *you* willing to be consistent for? Your answer will determine your future and will define who you are and who you will become.

Consistency Follows Your Innermost Vision

In the Proverbs 29:18 of The Holy Bible, we read "Where there is no vision, the people perish." I could not agree with this more. You are here on this earth to fulfill a mission that God has placed in your heart in the form of what we call talents and natural abilities. From these talents and abilities spring forth the vision of what you must do. When we turn our heads away from what is in our hearts and what we know to be true, we will *perish* emotionally, spiritually, and financially as well.

"I do what I have to do and not what I feel like doing is my formula for success." – *Charles I. Prosper*

13

Self Quiz – What Is Your Consistency IQ?

I know that one of the best way to learn is to learn by doing. As you read and understand the concepts and principles throughout this book, I thought that it would be helpful to include a self-test to gauge your understanding and readiness for the execution of the principles of persistence and consistency.

Do you understand the meaning of consistency? Would you know how to carry it out? Complete this self-inventory to find out. There are 10 statements, and they are presented in sets of three responses. Each response has a point value. Carefully read all three statements and then chose which one best describes your understanding of consistency. (In order not to ruin your book, I suggest that you photocopy the pages before taking the test.) Once photocopied, you can then write the point value on the line that is beside the response you have chosen.

What is Your Consistency IQ?

1. When I begin an important project, I
___ use a proven formula by a well-known success guru. (1)
___ create my own plan, write it down, and follow it daily. (3)
___ just begin and worry about a plan later. (2)

2. After joining a gym to get in shape, I
___ get a trainer to get me started if this is new to me. (3)
___ tell all of my friends and ask for their opinions. (1)
___ do what the other people in the gym are doing. (2)

3. I decide to write a book on a subject I'm passionate, I
___ wait for inspiration and then write non-stop. (1)
___ write for 1 hour a day whenever I can. (2)
___ commit to writing 1 hour daily, same-time same-place. (3)

4. I prepare to write for an hour when I get an urgent call, I
___ change my writing schedule to a different time. (2)
___ write for as long as I can, then I attend the situation. (3)
___ skip writing just for today and continue tomorrow. (1)

5. I decide to master real estate investing, I
___ hire a successful realtor who also owns property. (3)
___ teach myself using "how-to invest in real estate" books. (2)
___ wait until I'm sure the market is right. (1)

6. I want to know a new person whom I've begun dating, I
___ believe bad behavior will change on its own in time. (1)
___ pay attention to how they act in romantic situations. (2)
___ observe what they do repeatedly in everyday situations. (3)

7. I've been seriously thinking about going back to school, I
___ choose the school, curriculum, and enroll immediately. (3)
___ continue to analyze all of the pros and cons. (2)
___ wait until there is more time. (1)

8. My retirement plan is to save $1000 monthly for10 years, I
___ put different amounts into my savings each month. (2)
___ set it up as an automatic deduction to a savings account. (3)
___ wait until all of my bills are paid out. (1)

9. I wake up one morning, and I am "not in the mood," I
___ do something even though it's not much. (2)
___ skip my practice and make up for it tomorrow. (1)
___ tell my feelings how to feel and do it all anyway. (3)

10. I decide to become more patient with my family, so I
___ wait for a challenging situation to prove my patience. (2)
___ wait until I am in the mood to be patience. (1)
___ practice patient on every small occasion to do so. (3)

Score: 21–30, you really understand the meaning and practice of consistency; 11–20, you still need some practice in understanding the meaning of being consistent; 1–10, you haven't yet grasped the meaning and practice of consistency. Re-read chapter 11 - and press on with your goals.

"Stay with the intention and the joy of doing, and you will get there; in fact, once you are following the joy of doing, you have already arrived." – *Charles I. Prosper*

14

Consistency and Your "Burning Obsession"

Again in the classic book *Think and Grow Rich* by Napoleon Hill, there is a core concept expressed for success, which is the driving power behind consistency and at the same time *defines* the essence of persistence. This is what Napoleon Hill, as a "burning desire to win." On page 40, he writes,

> Every person who wins in any undertaking must be willing to burn his ships and cut all sources of retreat. Only by so doing can one be sure of maintaining that state of mind known as a BURNING DESIRE TO WIN, essential to success."

What Napoleon Hills calls a burning desire, I like to call a "burning obsession." Your burning obsession, in a word, is your passion. Your passion is your purpose and thus defines who you are and who you must become. You can know yourself by whatever consumes you day and night and compels you to use your recognized talents and all that which comes natural to you. I think that all of us know intuitively what we enjoy doing most and what we do naturally and with great ease. It is not that we don't know, it is that we have a hard time surrendering and trusting that we can succeed at doing our passion as our life's work. This self-doubt supresses our self-knowledge and puts us in a state of perpetual *wanting* to "discover our *real* life purpose."

We think what we want is not good enough or is not "practical" enough. There is nothing more practical than pursuing your passion because you won't give up and along the way, the *how* and the *what* will always be discovered. Your passion is your life, and life reveals itself to itself. Once you surrender and follow your heart, this trusting will show you how. As you move forward, this self-trust will transmute itself into anticipation, and from anticipation then to excitement, and from excitement ultimately to your day-and-night burning obsession. Trusting yourself and maintaining a single-minded laser-like focus is the key. Obstacles become challenges that you meet and willingly overcome in order to move on to the next and the next levels of success.

All Champions Have a Burning Obsession

All champions have a burning obsession to win or achieve a certain goal that they have determined to be absolutely necessary. This can be said of all of the greatest artists, writers, inventors, scientists, political activist, and humanitarians of history. They all have a burning obsession for something, and this burning obsession keeps them on course, where the ordinary-minded individual would have long since given up. People of greatness are visionaries. Their visions fuel them forward. They see beyond obstacles and continue boldly moving closer and closer to their purpose.

A. Schwartzenegger's Burning Obsession (Bodybuilding)

Arnold Schwartzenegger is one of the most complex, famous, and internationally well-known individuals around. By the time I finish prouncing the last syllable of his long and awkward last name, there is no doubt who we are talking about. In the title of this section, I say that his burning obsession was bodybuilding, but more accurately, bodybuilding was *one* of the first of his many burning obsessions, in all of which he became well-known and successful. He also went on to become successful in real estate investing, action movie-making, and politics. Schwartzenegger once said, "You can accomplish anything you want in life if you're willing to pay the price."

Schwarzenegger was born in Thal, Austria, a little village bording the city of Graz. Arnold had a dream and burning obsession to come to the United States since he was 10-years-old. He saw his passion for bodybuilding as his gateway to move to the U.S. to compete in bodybuilding contests.

In September of 1968, Schwartzenegger moved to the Venice, California, where he trained under fitness icon and promoter, Joe Weider. The greatest title in the world of bodybuilding is the Mr. Olympia, which in 1970 at age 23 he won for the first time in New York. Then through focus, commitment, dedication, and consistency, he went on to win this title of a total of seven times, making bodybuilding history.

When Schwarzenegger arrived to the U.S. from Austria, he spoke little or no English, so he enrolled in English classes at Santa Monica College in Santa Monica, California and so thereafter mastered the language. Still committed to his learning and advancement, he earned a BA by correspondence from the the University of Wisconsin-Superior. In 1979, he graduated with his degree in international marketing of fitness and business administration.

Before Arnold became successful in the movies and in politics, few people know that he was a fearless and focused entrepreneur and became very successful in business. Schwarzenegger was knowm to be a prolific goal-setter. He would have the habit of writing down his goals at the beginning of each year on index cards and then reviewing them daily; he would then take action and move forward toward their achievement. He would write, for example, such goals as "I intend to start a mail order business," or "I intend to buy a new car," and through consistent and relentless *action* would proceed to accomplish it.

Arnold become very effective with his ability to set goals and to consistently follow through with action. By age 30, Arnold Schwarzenegger was a millionaire well before he became famous as action movie star in Hollywood. He was first an entrepreneur by starting a series of succesful business ventures and then moving into *property* investments.

One of Schwarzenegger first business ventures was bricklaying. In 1968, with his close friend and fellow bodybuilder Franco Columbu, they took advantage of the increased demand for housing reconstruction following the 1971 San Fernando, California earthquake and together they started a bricklaying business. Schwarzenegger's marketing savvy and business acumen allowed them to earn enough money to parlay their profits into starting a mail order business targeting bodybuilders, which then they sold fitness-related equipment and instructional tapes.

Unlike the ordinary bodybuilders, Schwarzenegger always had his eye on the prize, and all the extra money that he earned had a *purpose* to move him to a higher level. Schwarzenegger took the profits from his mail order business and the winnings from his bodybuilding competions to *invest* in his first real estate venture – an apartment building which he purchased for $10,000. From the purchase of this first apartment building, Schwarzenegger would then go on to purchase a *number* of real estate holdings. His *first* million was made in real estate.

In 1995, along with fellow movie actors: Bruce Willis, Demi Moore, and Sylvester Stallone, Schwarzenegger, was one of the founding celebrities of the Planet Hollywood chain of international restaurants, which was modeled after the Hard Rock Café. Later, however, he severed his ties with the business in 2000, saying that the company had not produced the success he had hoped for. He said that he wanted to focus his attention on new US global business ventures and his movie career.

Schwarzenegger then invested in numerous other business ventures. He has significant ownership in an investment firm, Dimensional Fund Advisors. He is owner the Arnold's Sports Festival, which is a three-day expo that hosts thousands of international health and fitness experts. He owns the movie production company called Oak Productions, Inc, and he owns Fitness Publications, which is a joint publishing venture with Simon & Schuster. Notwithstanding all of his profitable business ventures, Arnold Schwarzenegger has commanded as much as $10 million dollars per movie. In 2002, LA Weekly said that Schwarzenegger had become the most famous immigrant in America, who "overcame a thick Austrian accent and transcended the unlikely background of bodybuilding to become the biggest movie star in the world in the 1990s."

We would be remiss not to examine one of the most notable and unexpected achievements of Schwarzenegger. In 1977 Arnold was introduced to Maria Shriver by news anchor Tom Brokaw at a party the night before the Robert F. Kennedy Pro-Celebrity Tennis Tournament in Forest Hills, New York. In case you don't already know, Maria Shriver is the niece of former President John F. Kennedy and Senator Robert F. Kennedy. The tournament was held annually in honor of her late uncle.

It is speculation that it was strategic or happenstance, but this introduction led to Schwarzenegger being positioned in the midst of great political power and influence. Arnold soon wooed and won the affection of this Kennedy, and on April 26, 1986, Arnold married Maria Shriver. In the undercurrents of this powerfully goal-oriented individual, Schwarzenegger had begun to move in a very specific direction.

In the wake of the recall election following Gray Davis, Schwarzenegger, on August 6, 2003 on The Tonight Show with

Jay Leno announce his candidacy for governor of California. In spite of the doubters and naysayers, on Oct. 7, 2003, this former bodybuilder from Austria and action movie star became Governor Arnold Schwarzenegger of California.

Steve Jobs' Burning Obsession (Personal Computing)

There is not a person alive who has not been touched by the world-changing technology of Apple Computer founder, Steve Jobs. Born 1955 in San Francisco, California and who died on October 5, 2011 at age 56. Jobs forever left his legacy on every man, woman, and child all over the globe.

When we speak of passion and commitment, Steve Jobs was the quintessential definition of the fusion of talent, consistency, and persistence. Steve Jobs had a passion for perfection with a ferocious drive and work ethic, which totally revolutionized the industries of personal computing, digital publishing, animated movies, music, tablet computing, and phones.

Steve Jobs was not born into wealth, to the contrary, he had very humble beginnings. His biological parents had him out of wedlock and so decided to put him up for adoption. Then Paul and Clara Jobs, a lower-middle-class couple, took him in and raised Steve as his adopted son.

Steve had an incredible curiosity and aptitude for electronics and technology; then his life was forever changed when, at 13 years of age, he met the most influential friend and accountability partner of his career, Stephen Wozniak, 18-year-old electronics wiz kid.

Wozniak became a part of the Homebrew Computer Club, who unnwittingly became the early pioneers of the personal computer. These brilliant amateurs would meet together to show off their prowess in building their own personal computers and writing their own software. This club started after the Altair 8800 personal computer kit came out in

1975.

Wozniak became adept at building his own computer board. Steve Jobs immediately saw that his friend's ability to assemble and build his own computer board could be marketed and sold to enthusiasts who were writing their own software and who didn't want the hazzle of assembling their own computers. Jobs convinced Wozniak that they could start a company with the purpose of marketing computers to software developers. Thus Apple Computer was born on April 1st of 1976.

The months following Job's impassioned brainstorm, both he and Wozniak spent hours assembling boards of the Apple I computers inside of Job's garage. They began to aggressivley sell their personal computers to the independent computer dealers in the area. Then there was a breakthrough. Wozniak developed an even better computer system, the Apple II, one that could support color graphics in a way that the world had never seen before. Jobs and Wozniak knew, without a shadow of a doubt, that this new advancement would be a revolutionary huge success.

Jobs realized that without venture capital, their idea would go no where. So he sought out and eventually convinced former Intel business executive Mike Markkula to invest $250,000 in Apple in January of 1977. Coincidentally, VisiCalc, the first commercially successful spreadsheet program had been developed. Virtually overnight, small business owners, accountants, and small business entrepreneurs, bought the Apple II in order do their business calculations at home.

Seeing the overwhelming response to the Apple II, Apple's investors decided to go public in December of 1980, which was only four years after Jobs had started the company. Steve Jobs net worth leaped to *over $200 million* by age 25.

In spite of the many technological innovations industries that Jobs introduced, what stands out most for me are the innovations of the iPod and the iPhone.

The iPod was the first digital music player, which made its debut on October 23, 2001. It totally replaced the cassette-playing Walkman, and became a commercial success from the day it was introduced. Instead of a dozen or so songs and tracks that a Walkman cassette player could handle, the latest 8 gigabyte iPod can hold up to 2000 songs, up to 7000 photos, and up to 8 hours of video. iPods have become very popular for listening to inspirational and instructional audio as well.

The iPhone was introduced at Macworld on January 9, 2007. The iPhone presented the touch screen technology, which has changed *world* culture. Tell me who do you know who does not have a touch screen smart phone in their pocket or purse?

Just look around and see how the world has changed. I have observed and have counted that at least 8 out of 10 people drive their cars while texting or moving the icons of their touch-screen phones with their middle or index fingers, held either on their steering wheels or in their laps, as they quickly look up and down (as though no one knows what they are doing.) I have seen people in restaurants, sitting at the same table, and all four people are using their touch screens, oblivious to each other's presence! People now walk on sidewalks and cross the streets with their eyes on their phones, *unconscious* to the world around them.

I remember one day that I was walking through one of the so-called "improverished" areas of Los Angeles, when a lady, sitting on a corner and on the sidewalk with her back propped against a building, asked me for spare change. As I reached into my pocket, her *cell phone* rang! She quickly pulls out her iPhone from her purse and answers, "Look, I'll call you back, okay! I'm busy." Seeing this, I quickly put my hand back in my pocket, turned around, and walked away.

At present, there are over 1 millions apps for the iPhone sold at the Apple Apps Store that have been created by software developers. *No other company* has been able to even get close to creating such a demand greater than the Apple platform.

At the time of his death in October of 2011, Steve Jobs was worth over $7 Billion. Talent, consistency, and persistence pay no matter how humble your beginnings may be.

Oprah Winfrey's Burning Obsession (TV News Media)

Oprah Gail Windfrey was born on January 29, 1954 in Kosciusko, Mississippi, a small farming community, to an unwed teenage mother and housemaid, Vernita Lee. Her mother broke up with her father, Vernon Winfrey, shortly after their first encounter. Oprah's humble beginnings were met with unfortunate experiences of sexual abuse by male relatives and acquaintances of her mother. Eventually, Oprah moved to Nashville, Tennessee to live with her father, who was a barber and small businessman. Her father was very strict and took her education very seriously. With her natural talent and her father's enthusiastic encouragement, Oprah became an honor's student at East Nashville High School. She was voted Most Popular Girl, and later joined her high school speech team and placed *second in the nation* for dramatic interpretation.

As a result of her winning an Oratory Contest, Oprah won a full scholarship to Tennessee State University, where she majored in communication.

When Oprah was only 17-years-old, she won the Miss Black Tennessee beauty pageant. As a result of this contest win, WVOL, a local Black radio station hired her as a part-time news anchor. She managed to work as a new anchor for the station during her senior year at East Nashville High and continued during the first two years at Tennessee State University.

Her media career began to move her to local television, where she was hired as the first Black female news anchor by Nashville's WLAC-TV.

In 1976, Oprah made a strategic move to Baltimore, Maryland, and was hired to co-anchor the six o'clock news.

On August 14, 1978, she was hired to co-host the local TV talk show at WJZ-TV's *People Are Talking*. With her signature personal style and passion for listening to others, the station kept her for eight years. Knowledge of her talent and charisma spread.

In 1983, Oprah moved to Chicago when she was given the opportunity to host Chicago's WLS-TV's *AM Chicago,* a 30-minute morning talk show. Only months after the first show aired on January 2, 1984, after Oprah had totally taken over, the show went from last place to first place in the nation, toppling the ratings of *Donahue,* which up until that time had been the highest rated talk show in Chicago.

Oprah signed a syndication deal with *King World,* a production company and syndicator of television programming in the United States.

On September 8, 1986, her show was renamed *The Oprah Winfrey Show,* and expanded to a full hour. *The Oprah Winfrey Show* drew in more than double *Donahue's* national audience, thus dethroning the once number-one daytime talk show host of America.

In spite of the fact that Oprah Winfrey was born into poverty in rural Mississippi and raised by a mother who worked as a housemaid and who received welfare assistance for the family, Winfrey became a self-made millionaire by age 32 when her talk show went nationwide. Her show generated so much revenue that she was in the position to *negotiate ownership* of the show and start her own production company.

At age 41, Oprah had a net worth of about $340 million. In 2006, Oprah was the highest paid television executive and entertainer in the U.S, earning approximately $260 million. As of 2014, it has been estimated that Oprah Winfrey has a net worth 2.9 Billion Dollars.

Bill Gates' Burning Obsession (Microsoft)

In Seattle, Washington, on October 28, 1955, to an upper middle-class family, was born the world-renowned computer mega-entrpreneur, Bill Gates.

At age 13, along with his childhood friend and later business partner, Paul Allen, Bill Gates began to show a talent and interest in computer programming while in middle school.

Bill and Paul began to experiment with the school teletype computers. Historically, for those too young to know what a teletype computer is, this was a sophiscated-looking typewriting machine that was used to communicate typed messages from point to point, that is, from one machine to another, something like the old-fashioned hole-punched ticker-tape stock machines used on Wall Street.

In 1970, at 15 years of age, with his friend Paul Allen, Bill Gates developed a computer program call the "Traf-o-Data," which was able to monitor traffic patterns in Seattle. They earned $20,000 with their first major business enterprise – quite a hefty sum for a 15-year-old in 1970. Bill wanted to go full-time into business as partners, but Gates' parents discouraged him in favor of finishing school and going to college to study law.

Bill enrolled in Harvard University in 1973, but he and Paul always stayed in contact. While at Harvard his passion remained for computer programming. In 1974, Gates wrote an article about the Altair Micro Computer 8800. Seeing his future in the world of computers, he immediately dropped out of Harvard in 1975 to give himself opportunity to the develop more software – his burning obsession.

Bill got back with Paul Allen. In 1975, they founded the Microsoft company. Bill and Paul realized that the manufacturers of the Altair Micro Computer 8800 would need new software for consumers to use to make their business and personal calculations. The amazing thing was that this dynamic duo had started writing many computer programs long before they knew about the Altair.

In 1980, Bill Gates, seeing that IBM was inching into the personal computer market, he developed MS-DOS as an operating system for the new IBM computers coming out. When Gates and Allen presented the compatible MS-DOS operating system to IBM, they sold it for a fee of $50,000. IBM also wanted to have the source code to MS-DOS, to manipulate changes and make improvements, but Gates refused. Instead, he decided to *license* the use of MS-DOS that would be *placed in* every IBM computer. This meant that everytime an IBM computer was sold, Microsoft would have to be paid a licensing fee. What was most brilliant about this strategy was that Gates knew that there would also be IBM clones, which later there were, and even the clone companies would have to pay a licensing fee for every computer that they sold.

By 1981, Microsoft's growth had exploded. Their employees increased from 25 to 128, and their revenues shot up from $4 million to $16 million.

In 1983, Microsoft went global, boasting offices in both Great Britain and Japan. At this time, 30 percent of the world's computers were running on Microsoft's software.

In 1983, his dear friend and partner Paul Allen was diagnosed with Hodgkin's disease, a cancer of the lymphatic system. Even though Paul's cancer went into remission a year later, he still decided to resign from the company.

Back in 1981, Microsoft and Apple had begun working together sharing many of their early innovations. Steve Jobs was already on the cutting edge developing a user-friendly graphical interface that the Macintosh is famous for. Gates quickly realized the threat that such a user-friendly interface would pose to Microsoft, so Gates "borrowed"many of the ideas that he gleaned from Jobs, and on November of 1985, he presented the graphical interface "Windows." A nasty court fight ensued between Gates and Jobs.

In the end, Microsoft prevailed. It was decided that, though the graphical interfaces of Windows and the Apple Macintosh were similar, each individual function were distinctly different.

In 1986, Bill Gates went public with Microsoft with an intial public offering of $21 per share. Since Gates held 45 percent of the company's 24.7 million shares, he became an instant millionaire at age 31. At this time, Gates owned, $234 million of Microsoft's $520 million.

In 1987, Bill Gates became a billionaire as soon as the stock raised to $90.75 a share giving him a net worth of $1.25 Billion.

In 1999, as stock prices increased even more, Gates's wealth briefly surpassed a whopping $101 Billion.

Gates, who stepped down from Microsoft in 2006, currently holds in 2015 a net worth estimated at 79.2 billion. At this stage of his life, he and his wife Melinda Gates are involved in worldwide philanthropy through their various international charitable foundations.

Precious Few Have a Burning Obsession

It appears that the key to a burning obsession is *surrender* and *belief in yourself.* If you notice that in the bios of all of these great achievers, one thing remains a common thread, and that is their ability to take immediate and decisive action. No matter what, they just keep moving. They move precisely and quickly once their vision is glimpsed. Their fast and forceful forward motion leaves them little time or room for doubt and indecision. They are all risk-takers, but their risks are predicated on who they are and who they have chosen to be. They trust themselves and this self-trust is rewarded by realizing the vision that they had maintained of themselves.

*"There is nothing more important than
what you choose to do right now."* –
Charles I. Prosper

15

Self Quiz # 2– Getting Off Track/On Track

Part of early mastery of consistency of any new and important project is the understanding that there will be those times when the unexpected happens and we are thrown off our schedule and routine. This is normal. Life happens. It is not so much that the unexpected becomes the problem but our preparation and knowledge of how to handle it.

Complete this inventory to find out your readiness to handle yourself when you are thrown off your game plan. Circle the word to the right as it applies to you and what you would do. (Again, I would suggest you photocopy this quiz.)

Quiz #2 - How Do You Handle Getting Off Track?

1. I become angry and frustrated if I oversleep and am late to go to the gym:

   Never   Rarely   Sometimes   Often   Always

2. I accept a dinner invitation with my friends and omit to tell them I am on a special low fat diet:

   Never   Rarely   Sometimes   Often   Always

3. I decide to save up the money for the down payment on a real estate property, so I tell all of my friends:

Never   Rarely   Sometimes   Often   Always

4. I consult with a professional or an expert in areas that are new to me:

Never   Rarely   Sometimes   Often   Always

5. I write 1 hour each day on a book I am writing; when I can't write an hour, I will write 15 or 20 minutes:

Never   Rarely   Sometimes   Often   Always

6. I write 1 hour each day on a book I am writing; if I can't write an hour today, I'll skip and write 2 hours tomorrow.

Never   Rarely   Sometimes   Often   Always

7. I create a detailed plan of how I will remain consistent for at least the first 30 days of a new project.

Never   Rarely   Sometimes   Often   Always

8. I spend some quiet time visualizing the successful achievement of my goal.

Never   Rarely   Sometimes   Often   Always

9. I believe in myself and I know that if I decide to do something, I will achieve it.

Never   Rarely   Sometimes   Often   Always

10. I blame luck, circumstances, and others when things don't go for me as planned.

Never   Rarely   Sometimes   Often   Always

1. Write a sentence that describes how you would like to change your approach to being more consistent.   Start it with "I resolve to..."

2. List the benefits of creating a plan to become more consistent.

3. List the obstacles to your mind that are preventing you from becoming more consistent.

4. Circle the items on the above list that are based on your past experience with being inconsistent. Make the decision to change those thoughts starting now.

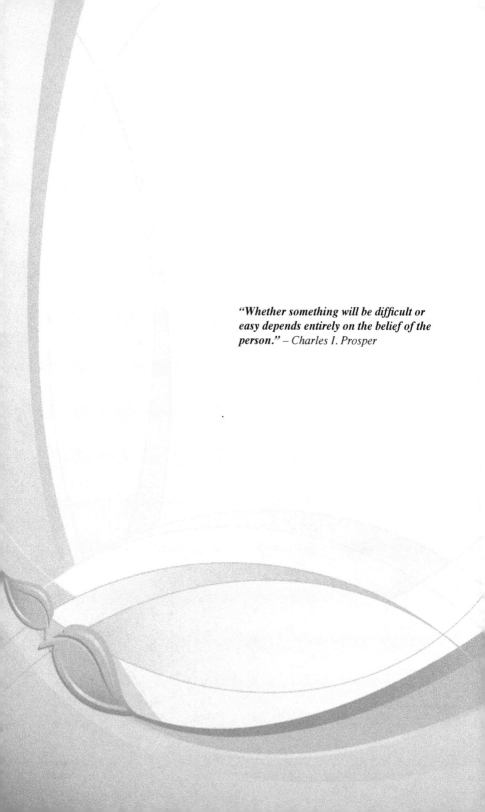

"Whether something will be difficult or easy depends entirely on the belief of the person." – *Charles I. Prosper*

16

Self-Quiz #3 – Avoiding Procrastination

When we procrastinate we are practicing the art of postponing achievement. By allowing procrastination to take over, we increase the perception of that which must be done is either overwhelming or impossible "at this time." This is how you feel immediately after you have procrastinated and have missed out on an opportunity to move forward and succeed. It is likely that you feel disappointed in yourself and ashamed that you didn't have more discipline to do what should have been done.

　　Can you resist and overcome the tendency and insidious habit of procrastination? The exercises below are designed to give you practice in realizing and overcoming procrastination and help you to develop your power to decide and take action no matter what.

Quiz #3 - How Do You Handle Procrastination?

1.　It is tax time, and April 15th is approaching in two week. Your procrastination response might be,

But instead you,

2. You have to get up at 4:00 a.m. today and go to the gym. Your procrastination response might be,

But instead you,

3. You have stayed away from high-fat high-calorie foods for a week, and someone has just offered you a glazed doughnut. Your procrastination response might be,

But instead you,

4. Starting your new website has been 3 weeks overdue. Your procrastination response might be,

But instead you,

5. You would like to invite that pretty co-worker for lunch with you one afternoon. Your procrastination response might be,

But instead you,

6. You have been putting off all morning writing down your real estate investment plan. Your procrastination response might be,

But instead you,

7. You think that you have to *finish* reading that how-to book on success *before* taking action now on your business idea. Your procrastination response might be,

But instead you,

8. After many years of waiting, this is the summer you will learn how to swim. Your procrastination response might be,

But instead you,

9. You need you see a doctor about unusual chest pains you have been experiencing. Your procrastination response might be,

But instead you,

10. It's time to plan for your retirement. Your procrastination response might be,

But instead you,

"Massive positive action is the second step to achieving any goal." – *Charles I. Prosper*

17

Self Quiz #4 – The 10 Principles of Consistency

I believe that simplicity is at the core of understanding any endeavor. There are those who take something simple and make it look complex as well as there are others who take something complex and explain it in simple terms. This quiz will gauge your understanding of the 10 principles of consistency.

Quiz #4 - Do You Understand the 10 Principles?

1. Do you start a new endeavor without clearing defining what it is that you want to achieve?

2. Are you unclear idea of the behaviors that you must consistenly carry out that will move you toward your goal.

3. Do you depend totally on yourself and avoid consulting with experts or experienced people with an important goal?

4. Do you take your time before starting a new goal.

5. Do you become surprised and frustrated when you notice that starting something new requires unusual effort?

6. Whenever you get off track, do you find it difficult getting back on track?

7. Do you become impatient when you don't see immediate results?

8. If a planned routine is interrupted, do you just skip the practice entirely and "make up" for it the next day?

9. Do you ever ask yourself why are you going through all of this trouble?

10. If the going gets too rough, do you just quit and try something else?

If you have answered yes to more than half of these questions, the chances are that you haven't spent much time thinking about what makes a person consistent. Your misconceptions are distracting you from realizing what you need to do in order to be and remain consistent. Try the following exercises to help you.

1. Make a list of those times when you have remained consistent and were able to achieve what you set out to do. These can be simple things like organizing your desk, getting to work earlier,

or spending more time with your children. Don't be afraid to reach back and remember the simplest occasions of your succesful consistency. List as many of those times as you can remember.

2. Focus on what you need to do to repeat the consistency of the times that you were successful with the items listed above.

3. List the qualities of super-consistent people.

4. List the qualities of super-achievers.

5. In lists 3 and 4, circle the qualities that appeal to you. Strive to achieve them in your daily life.

"When you don't know what to do – do only what you can do, and see what happens. Do more of what works and less of what doesn't until you goal is inevitably achieved." – Charles I. Prosper

CHAPTER 18

Self-Quiz #5 – How Low Moods Affect Focus

No matter how determined and powerful we think ourselves to be, there will always be those occasional times when we suddenly find ourselves in a "low" mood. Low moods can happen through a temporary illness, which lowers our resistence to stress. Something as common as a cold or the flu, can weaken our persistence and fight. As humans, we all go through cyclical emotional biorythms; some would say that we are even affected by the gravitational pull of the full moon. Regardless of the reason, it is how we recognize and handle these low periods, which will determine our continued success.

Quiz #5 - How Do You Handle Low Moods?

1. Are you immediately aware when you are in an atypical low mood?

2. Do you consider yourself a regularly moody person or only an occasional one?

3. Do others notice it when you are in a low mood?

4. Look at the list below. Check all those that apply to you when you are in a low mood:

_____ indecisive

_____ doubtful

_____ indifferent

_____ impatient

_____ judgemental

_____ cynical

_____ despondent

5. How do you typically behave when you are in a low mood?

6. When you are in a low mood, how do you snap yourself out out of it?

7. List the type of events can create a low mood for you?

8. List those things that you can do, that are able to change your low mood into a good mood - things that can bring you up?

9. How quickly do you resort to doing those positive things that will change your mood from negative to positive?

10. Do you ever make important decisions when you are in a low mood?

11. Do you postpone making important decisions until you are in a more positive state?

12. Do you tell your feelings how to feel, and tell your thoughts what to think?

"Luck is a factor of what I do or I fail to do in a timely and consistent manner." – *Charles I. Prosper*

19

Q & A Interview with Charles Prosper

I have had some of the best discussions on consistency with my dear friend, Joseph Daniel, who will do the honor of interviewing me on the subject of consistency today.

Joseph Daniel Interviews Charles Prosper on Consistency

C. P. Joseph, it's good to have you here today. And so you're going to interview me on the subject of consistency. Correct?

J.D. You're right.

C. P. Okay. So this is the idea we'll follow. We have some questions we're going to address, and then we're going to go look at some important topics and just let this whole thing flow. So, you can start with the first basic question, and let's see what we come up with.

J. D. Okay. So, Mr. Prosper, why is consistency – I mean the subject of consistency so important?

C. P. Well, the thing is that people believe that just knowing so-called formulas and the secrets of success is what's important. I've even written a book called The 12 Laws of Success. I think it's a very good book, but it is worthless unless a person understands consistency, because consistency is the litmus test. This is the point where you do what you say that you know.

It is not only the point of doing what you say that you know, but it is doing it in a way that is repeated as you move forward closer and closer to your goal. And consistency is something that doesn't happen by default. I don't believe people are born with the tendency to be consistent.

J. D. This brings me to my next question. Why is it that so many people are not consistent?

C. P. In a word – it's the D word – Discipline. People are very uncomfortable with discipline, and discipline is at the core of consistency. Getting yourself to do something that is contrary to inertia is what we can call discipline, because discipline breaks inertia.

Let's give an example. A person wants to lose weight. And they're used to eating their donuts, their fried chicken, their McDonald's French fries, or whatever it is and they usually eat. They think, "Oh, I'm 50 pounds overweight; I need to do something different!" But they have gotten into a mental state of pleasure that's to their disadvantage.

Now, to go to the other way, you have to go against something that is already set in momentum – which is the habit of poor eating. So when you try to reverse the habit, there's resistance and you have to break this resistance through that which we called discipline.

Because discipline is not comfortable, the first step to being consistent is to make a plan, which is in contrary to what you were doing before. And to be contrary to what you were doing before is something that is uncomfortable. Most people really find change painful, and few people welcome pain or discomfort.

So it's like no one wants to pay the price of change. The price is discomfort in order to be able to break the barrier of resistance, which sits before the discipline that you will have to execute.

J. D. So, in other words, you're saying that it is the litmus test that determines whether you're disciplined or not.

C. P. Yes. In theory, you can say, "I'm going to do this. I'm going to do that." That's all theoretical. You can say, "I just went to this seminar, and I learned the seven steps on how to lose weight, or I learned the 10 secrets of how to become wealthy, and I just have to do A, B, C, and D. And I understand these principle one hundred percent. I've got it!"

J. D. Right.

C. P. Okay. So, understanding is fine. Knowing is fine. But that's not enough. It is not until you do – that the change happens. And it's not until you do what you say you know that the litmus test happens.

So, nothing happens until you do what you say that you know. And doing what you say that you know involves a change that is uncomfortable, painful, and difficult. And most people are not willing to submit themselves to this; that's why consistency is rarely seen because most people don't like discomfort and will avoid it at all cost.

Most people like their comfort zone, and consistency goes outside of the comfort zone.

J. D. So then, how does the person get out of their comfort zone and become consistent?

C. P. Well, they have to have a willingness to suffer. They have to be willing to surrender to the fires of change. And not many people are willing to do that.

J. D. Right.

C. P. They have to be willing to be crucified—to be crucified from their old thinking to be resurrected into a new way of thinking.

J. D. That's deep.

C. P. You can't avoid pain in order to grow, and that is what a consistency involves. Change must move in a different direction in order to grow in the way that you have seen in your vision. But change is not pleasant. Change is not easy.

Change involves pain, but pain is necessary. Pain is a necessary element to change that purifies you of your bad habits so that you can get to the point where you no longer feel the pain because you're now purified and then it has become a new way of living.

So, you go through a stage of feeling pain, but that pain is temporary. Discipline is the pain, but discipline is temporary. Once you have purified yourself of your old habits, new habits are replaced, and now you are enjoying a new way of life.

But to pass to that stage, you have to pass through the stage of pain, and that's why consistency is so difficult.

J. D. Just like somebody saying, "I want to go to heaven but I don't want to die."

C. P. Exactly. Exactly. That is exactly what it's like. And I say that as a rule, the majority or the average person is not consistent. The average person is mediocre. In fact, in terms of mediocrity, majority always rules.

So, to see a consistent person who is consistently carrying out his or her goals is something that's not seen quite commonly because if you look at the general population of people, the majority of people don't want the pain of change.

They want the change, but they don't want the pain that comes before the change, and so they procrastinate, which keeps anyone from doing what must be done.

This is how procrastination works. A person who wants to

start a business says, "Well, I want to start a business, so I'll get a degree in business from college first." And so they get a degree in business from a 4-year college. (Of course, they could've started any time.) However, after obtaining their undergraduate degree, they'll say, "Oh, no, I'm not ready. I need an MBA. I need a masters in Business Administration." They get the MBA, and then say, "Well, I'm not quite ready yet. I need to get some post doctorate studies, and then maybe I'll be ready."

After entering into a doctorate business program, they discover these fascinating business seminar workshops that guarantee to show people how to become rich and successful, "Well, once I get the information from these seminars, then I'll be ready."

So goes the person who the mindset of avoiding the pain of change; that person will use all types of devices to avoid taking action – even when, on the surface the device may be something that's good, such as accumulating formal education.

But accumulating education in the wrong way, a way that is set up to avoid taking action can be pernicious and self-defeating to a person.

J.D. Interesting. So then again, it brings me back to my question that it is one thing to want to be consistent, and it is entirely another thing to actually stay consistent. How does a person stay consistent?

C. P. It is predicated on why a person wants to be consistent in the first place. The "why" of change has to be greater than the "what must be done" in order to change.

For example, you want to have your family with a better life, and you know that the only way that you're going to get there is by saving your money, investing in real estate, foregoing pleasures that's going to use up your money, and ignore the temptations that other people will fall into of having a good time and spending not spending money wisely.

So you're going to have to forego lots of the distractions, diversions, and pleasures that most people would say "I deserve to have this" as their justification for mindless spending. And the way that you stay focused is simple. At nighttime, look into the eyes of your children, and see how they depend up on you to give them a better life, and then you can start to see the importance of your consistency.

The importance of your consistency to take care of your children makes you willing to go through any amount of pain and discomfort because taking care of your children is much greater than the pain, discomfort and temporary suffering that you might have to put yourself through.

Most people don't have a why that is important enough to keep them consistent. It's more like a futile flight of fancy, as you like to say. They say, "Oh, I would like to save up and invest in real estate. Oh, I would like to lose weight. Oh, I would like to get a college degree," but there's no fire inside of their belly. There's no willingness to suffer. There's no willingness to be purified by the pain of change.

There is pain in change. Make no mistake about it. You can't get around the fact that there's always pain in change. But I didn't say that pain was bad; it's just an experience that makes you more worthy of what you say that you want.

Pain is not welcomed, but it is necessary. And, in the ultimate sense of wisdom, pain is a good thing, if you stay with it long enough. Pain will give you the reward of being its companion, if you stay with it long enough.

J.D. So, can we definitely say that regarding the subject of consistency, it is one of the most important elements that distinguishes a successful person from a non-successful one?

C.P. Absolutely. Positively. In fact, a person who is consistent–let's step back a bit… If a person doesn't have a plan, but if a person has the *intention* to achieve something without a plan, the consistent focus of the intended goal will *lead* the person to the ways and means of the plan to follow.

With strong intention and consistent action, you really don't need to see everything that you will need to do in the future from start to finish.

People who sit back on their laurels and rest back on their high chairs intellectualizing all the formulas and plans that need to be done, that need to be presented out to them into the far distant future before they are willing to take any steps, are the people who are cowards.

People of courage step out, and as the Bible says, "They move by faith and not by sight." So, with this kind of consistency, they can continue to move forward even without a detailed plan, even without a formula, even without a bevy of motivational teachers and motivational books, tapes, and audio how-to instruction.

I have at last come to the conclusion that most motivational speakers are totally *unnecessary* – including me – if you really intend on following your dream, your passion, and are willing to do whatever it takes and willing to surrender to the pain of change.

You don't need *anybody* for that. A little orientation might be good, but in the final analysis, the only person that you need is *you*, your willingness and your ability to take action repeatedly, again and again and again, relentlessly, non-stopping until the point where you can see your own light and your own way.

J.D. So I see that from your discussion. Consistency is the fine thread that weaves through all successful endeavors and all successful people.

C.P. All successful people know consistency. There's one thread that I have observed as I've studied some of the most successful people around, and that is the fact that they continue no matter what – after they first get the vision, they start to move and they move quickly with it. They don't wait. They don't procrastinate. They don't need any more inspiration other than the vision that they have been given. They move quickly with it, and they continue to move.

Listen to what I said. They move – I didn't say they move, and they stop. I didn't say they move, stop, and go to a seminar or read a book, study, analyze, or think again, before they take action. I didn't say that. I said that they move quickly, and they continue to move. That is the formula, if there is a formula, which is the ability to move and continue to move.

This is definition of consistency, and it is the guarantee of success because success can be defined by consistent movement toward that what you see and feel in your heart.

J.D. I like that.

C. P. So, that is exactly how it works.

J.D. So then it brings me back to the question of, say, a person who wants to lose, say, about eight pounds and they say they want to exercise. So, on Monday they go to the gym and eat they properly and they exercise, but then they skip Tuesday, Wednesday, and Thursday. So they say on Friday will make up for the three skipped days by working out three-times as hard. Is that possible?

C. P. No, because you can't replace time. Once time has been lost, it's lost. You can't replace yesterday because yesterday is no longer there. Today is a new day. You can't add on to a day that you never did.

So there is no such thing as replacing a missed day. It is, like you call it, a futile flight of fancy. It's like when we've talked about savings. We've had this discussion many times. If a person says he wants to save $500 a month, so he'll save, let's say, $500 this month and $500 next month, that's a thousand; but then he skips a month, and then skips *another* month.

Okay. Now they say, "I'm going to make up for skipping those two months by placing a thousand dollars extra the following month. It's *impossible* to "to make up" those skipped months because if you're saving $500 a month for six months and you skip three, you will only have$1500.

You're supposed to have at least $3,000 after 6 months of consistent saving. So even if you replace $1500 in the 6th month, you're going to have only $3,000 – but, consistently speaking, you were supposed to have had $4,500.

J.D. Yes, that's right!

C. P. So, no, you can't replace money because that is not the *same* money. And you can't replace that day missed because it's not the *same* day. The people who allow themselves the delusion that a day *can* be wasted are missing out on the understanding of how consistency works.

Every day is the day that counts. And if you miss it, you're starting all over again the next day because every day counts. A person moves forward through faith. It is the *doing* that creates the success not the *knowing* that creates the success.

People have it backwards. People would think that the more they know, the more successful they would become. I say, the more you do, the more success you will experience because you will know and discover the *right* things instead of the *formulas* that are artificially given for you to follow that don't most times even fit in with your life.

You have to have *custom-made* plans that *develop themselves* as you go along, and only you can do this by consistently moving forward and consistently moving forward a little more; that's the way things happen.

I think that in the total population of people, those who are truly consistent, are probably only about 5 or 10%.

Consistency like anything else is a *learned* trait. I think it a learned trait. We're not born with it, but we learn and develop it over time. When we understand its importance, we give ourselves to it completely.

So the more we are consistent, the more we are successful and the more we understand how it makes us successful. Consistency and success are interchangeable and inseparable.

So consistency is the path and at once it reveals the path. It is the path that we travel, and it reveals the higher paths that we need to continue to travel.

J.D. Can you give us a little bit of a historical perspective of how you arrived at the idea that consistency is so crucial to endeavors as people?

C. P. I spent many years accumulating knowledge, getting ready to do, getting ready to act until I had an epiphany. I don't know if it was one day I realized, but soon I realized that this getting-ready-to-act is not acting. So I asked myself, "Who am I kidding?"

J.D. That's deep.

C. P. Who was I kidding? This getting ready to act is not acting, so why am I postponing the thing that's going to make me successful.

So, I just began to act, without being 100% ready, and then I learned by doing; I learn as I went along.

And I discovered this approached worked with a business enterprise I started. I realized this approached worked when I went back to graduate school later in life and obtained a Masters in Psychology. I learned how to get into great physical shape by just beginning.

I did all of this without extreme preparation, knowledge, consultations, seminars, lots of meditating, and all the excessive visualizing, that you are supposed to do before taking action. Some preparation is fine, but if taken to the extreme, it will postpone you from taking action. If you do too much preparation, you eventually become addicted to the preparation process. You become paralyzed from acting.

It's okay to study what you plan to do, talk to an expert, visualize, write your goal on a card, put it on your mirror, read it as much as you like, but do this sparingly. I believe that these things should be done moderately, like 5% of your time invested. The 95% part is the taking action. Most people have it backwards. They spend 95% of their time visualizing, meditating, affirming, writing on index cards, going to seminars, reading books and just analyzing the plans to death.

I call this paralysis of analysis. You can do so much of this until you get into a state where enough is never enough.

The problem lies when we start accumulating knowledge to such a degree that we get to the point where it's never enough. You're not ready because there's another book that's coming out next year. You're not ready because there's another workshop that's going to be held in three months; so you never ready.

I told you about my friend Winston who developed a very

successful dental lab. He came here from Ecuador when he was about 22. He used to work for me when I had my balloon and party shop. He didn't speak any English at the time.

He said that he had been trained in his country as a dental technician. He made the implants and false teeth and oral replacement stuff for the dentists. He told me that he wanted to start his own business here in Los Angeles. Now, me, in all of my infinite wisdom, thinking I'm going to save him some frustration, said to him, "Oh, Winston, I don't know. You're not able to speak the language. You don't know anybody here. You don't have any connections. You don't have any money. How can you start a business like that here?"

He worked for me about a year, and later got a job working in a dental lab. I lost track of him.

Fast forward 26 years later, I am sitting at a table with my daughter Luzemily in an open air café of a popular shopping center, when Winston and his wife Linda walk up to me and greet us with smiles and hugs. Long story short, Winston and his wife Linda during this 26-year-interval had established a multi-million dollar dental lab business in Simi Valley, California. They had just bought their second home, paid out the building where he operates his business, and has hundreds of thousand dollars worth of dental equipment in his office.

While staying over as a guest at his palatial estate, I asked him, "Winston, how did you do it?" I asked, "Did you read a lot of books on success? Did you go to a lot of business seminars?" He then responded with a quizzical look on his face, "No, I never read any books or attended any seminars." I then asked, "Well, did you set a lot of big goals? Did you write them on cards? Did you visualize them?" He said, "No, I never did any of that." He just took action! He just took consistent action! He didn't ever plan. He didn't visualize day and night. He didn't write it on cards. He didn't put it on the mirror. He never knew who Napoleon Hill was; he just did it.

And then that opened my eyes to the fact that most people just *know* too much, or they think that they don't know enough to just begin and to take action.

In fact, I can even predict the probability of the *lack* of success that a person is likely to encounter, as a direct correlation to how many books, audios, tapes, seminars he continues to read and listen to right now, which is impeding the his ability to take action because while he or she is listening to the plethora of audios and watching videos and going to seminars and reading books and talking about their goals, they're taking all of their time *away* from taking action.

This the irony of it all, the more time you spend collecting information, the less likely you're going to take action. You need to do this information-collecting sparingly. And in the case of my friend Winston, he didn't do it at all. He just took action and learned as he went along.

If you listen to the success-formula-promoting motivational gurus, they'll tell you all the things that you will need before you can even consider that you have a viable goal. What is it that they usually tell you, Joseph?

J.D.   It needs to be specific. It needs to be measurable. It needs to attainable. It needs to be realistic. It needs to be time based, and we need to develop a strategic plan and tactical plan to achieve the objective.

C. P. Now, that goes out the window when you meet somebody like Winston. So, now what do you do? How do you tell Winston he wasn't supposed to be successful because he didn't do all of these things? So, what made him successful since he didn't do all of the things that the success leaders say that we all need to do? The difference is he just took consistent action…

J.D. Consistent action.

C. P. And learned along the way. Life gave him the plan that he needed as he learned along the way. This is what I too have discovered that it is the way that it all works. Most people don't want to do this. Most people need the comfort and security of having somebody tell them "these are the steps that you need to take."

J.D. And it may be different for every individual just like our fingerprints are different.

C. P. It is different from every individual. I mean, it's like this guy Nick Vujicic. He's this motivational speaker who was born without arms and legs. Can you imagine if he gave us a seminar on how to be successful? Maybe I would to have to divest myself of my arms and my legs because that's how he did it!

So, we can't follow the exact formula of anybody because everybody's situation is so different. So the thing is, success formulas don't work.

I'm sorry. Success formulas don't work. They just don't work. They might be interesting and entertaining, but they don't work because there's no one-size-fits-all success formula, a set pattern for everyone at all times.

The success formula for me at age 20 is not the same success formula that would work for me now in past 50. It is not the same formula.

So even at different stages of your life, the success formula for the same individual will change according to his or circumstances throughout the course of his or her lifetime.

A success formula for a single person is going to be different from the success formula for a married man with a wife and two kids, would you agree?

J.D. I couldn't agree with you more.

C. P. So, we can't have a one-size-fits-all success formula. It has to be something that is discovered through action. What kind of action? Consistent…

J.D. Consistent action.

C. P. Life will reveal itself to the person who trusts that life has a secret to reveal to them.

And life will reveal it to you if you consistently move forward without demanding you have the answers upfront.

You have to *earn* the answers, and you earn the answers by taking action, by having faith, by doing what you need to do right now. Because what you need to do right now is different from what you will need to do later; it evolves out of what you do now. You don't get to know what you need to do later yet because you haven't done what you need to do now.

So, there's no such thing as success formula.

J.D. So then what I'm getting here is that all motivational speakers attempt to create a wave.

C. P. Yes, we know that the surfer can learn to *ride* the wave, but we know that he cannot *create* a wave. And likewise I say that no one can create light in you. If you don't come with the spark, no one can give you the spark of light.

Light or inspiration comes from God, however you may define the All-That-Is or the Organizing Intelligence of the Universe. God gives the spark inside the moment the person thinks, "Ah, maybe my life could be different if I take action." That's the spark.

Now, the motivational guru appears before the person, and with his words it become like bellows which blow on the spark inside of that person who has become ready. Now his spark heats up and becomes white-hot.

If there's no spark there initially, the motivation speaker can speak until he is blue in the face and nothing will happen within that person.

Think of it this way. If I go to a supermarket and search the shelves where a bag of charcoal can be found and I slit open the side of the bag, several cubes of charcoal fall out. I cannot blow on that store charcoal and expect to heat without it first already having been lit. So it is when it comes to "motivating" a person. The spark or the willingness must first be there, or no amount of motivational pep talk will take any effect.

J.D. I can imagine how a football coach would struggle with a guy who has no talent whatsoever and no interest to play football whatsoever and tried to make him into a pro football player.

C. P. Yes. It doesn't work like that. And some of the people who delude themselves the most are therapists, many teachers, social workers, and counselors, who believe that they can give light, a spark, or hope to a person.

I do not believe that inspiration is given from one human to another. The word "in-spire" says it all. The word inspiration comes from the Latin route, which literally means a "breath from within."

Inspiration is something that comes from a person's inner experience with him or herself as how they relate to God because God infuses us with the hope that makes us feel, "I need help". When the person feels "I need help," then the teacher appears. When the student is ready, the teacher appears. It's not the other way around.

So motivation happens first from within, and it may start as a little spark, or an awakening. When anyone helps another person it will be to *fan the spark*, which is already there.

A person must come to the teacher *already* with the spark and say, "Show me how I can keep this up," and so the teacher blows the encouragement on that person.

The person still has to walk the path. This person still has to take the action. The teacher can blow the inspiration, can fan the flame hotter and hotter, but the person still has to walk the walk by him or her self. He still has to walk his own path. The teacher will heat him up, and then the teacher will go in the other direction, allowing that person to walk his path alone.

J.D. So then it comes to my mind that the subject of consistency is more like the road less traveled.

C. P. Exactly. "Two roads converged in a woods," as Robert Frost said in his classic poem, "but one took the road that was less traveled, and that made all the difference."

The road less traveled is where the consistent people walk. So that was the road that was less traveled, but it all made the difference.

That message of Robert Frost's poem was very clear. When you take the road less traveled by, the road that not many people want to travel, that is the road that will make all the difference.

So, I would say, in conclusion, that to be consistent, you must have a clear vision of something that you are moving toward that's much more important than the discomfort that you need to go through to get there.

The value of that what you seek has to be greater than the temporary pain or discomfort that you would need to pass through in order to get there. Your willingness to do it is the litmus test.

You can "say" you're willing, but it's not until you "do" that the litmus test is proven.

So theory is one thing, understanding is another, but it is not until you *do* what must be done, that things begin happen.

So, I think that with this we will conclude for today. I really enjoyed talking to you, my good friend.

J.D. And I want to thank you for giving me the opportunity to interview you and to learn from you as well.

C. P. It was my pleasure. I had no idea what I was going to say, so I've learned a lot here myself.

J.D. Thank you, sir.

C. P. Thank you.

"You are born again every time you wake up." – Luzemily Prosper (spoken at 11-years-old)

20

Q & A Interview with Luzemily Prosper

Today I have the pleasure of interviewing my brilliant 16-year-old daughter, Luzemily Prosper. Luzemily can hold her own when it comes to explaining and understanding the principles of success and consistency. At 11-years-old, she wrote her first book, *The Sayings of Luzemily, the 7-Year Old Sage* (Global Publishing Company, 2010), available on Amazon.com or BarnesandNoble.com.

Charles Prosper Interviews Luzemily on Consistency

C. P.   Hello, everybody. This is yours truly, Charles Prosper. And today, I have the honor of having my beautiful daughter, Luzemily Prosper, who is going to give her take on why consistency is important for young people. Now, when I say young people, let me kind of clarify what we're talking about. How old are you now, baby?

L. P.   Sixteen.

C. P.   Okay. We've talked about consistency many times. Have we not?

L. P. Yes, we have.

C. P. And you have a pretty good grasp of its importance, shall I say, correct?

L. P. Yes, I do.

C. P. Okay. So, you're going to direct this to the audience of young and older because this is a subject that everybody can grasp. But the earlier we can understand the importance of consistency, the better. So, I'll just start up by asking you, baby. Why is consistency especially important for young people?

L. P. Well, consistency not only is important for younger people, the younger generation, it's important for everyone. It's what really keeps us on track. Without consistency, everything would just be a mess. I mean, imagine planning something without writing it down or thinking about it.

Basically, consistency is what keeps us together. It's the plan of our life. To be consistent is staying on track with what you need to do, what you want to do, and what you want to fulfill. To be consistent is being true to yourself.

C. P.   For example, how important is consistency when a person – a student needs to make good grades and to study? How does...

L. P.   Well obviously, being consistent with your studies is like the number one thing. Usually, you hear a lot of procrastination; you hear a lot of neglecting of work that is put it off. A project is due in two weeks, and they end up doing it in the last few days of the weekend.

When you're consistent, you avoid the stress of having to do things at the last minute. Instead of having to wait for the last two days of your assignment to do your work, you do a little bit each and every day and at a certain time.

After you get back home from school, you start to work. If you have any chores to do, do those first, whatever you need to do. But you've got to set yourself a time to do your work, to work on your project. You work on things little by little. It doesn't have to be everything all at one moment. That way, you're calm about it, and you don't stress yourself out about it.

If you do a little bit more each day, you could finish it ahead of time, and then you could just relax the rest of the way.

C. P.   Now, why is it that people procrastinate? Because the opposite of consistency or the enemy of consistency is procrastination. Why do people procrastinate?

L. P.   I believe people procrastinate because they feel like their time is being used inefficiently, which takes them from other things that they would rather do. Like, let's say, if a kid wants to go to some kind of movie or has some kind of plans for fun, they'll put off the work so that they could have the fun. But by doing that, you're getting caught up with a lot of work, which is piling up and piling up.

I hate to say it, but some kids – a lot of kids are lazy. Most of them would rather be playing games or talking to their friends, things they feel are a lot more important than finishing their work each and every day.

C. P. So, you're pretty much saying is that one of the reasons why people procrastinate is because they don't want to do what is unpleasant?

L. P.   They don't want to do what's unpleasant, so they put it off to the last minute and then just wing it.

C. P. Or try to wing it.

L. P.   Or try to wing it at least. But then they fail.

C. P.   And so, then in general, why do think that most young people are not consistent? Is it because they don't want to face the difficult task that they have to face, and it's easier for them to just

to pretend like it's not important and do something else that's fun?

L. P. Yeah. It's like, you say, they'd rather be doing something fun. Kids find that schoolwork is sometimes boring. And too many kids just want to have fun. And I understand that, you want to enjoy yourself more than you want to do your work.

But you have to face the reality that everyone has to do some things that they don't want to do.

C. P. You're right.

L. P. So, instead of starting off by talking with friends, going out and doing all that, first, finish what you've got to do a little bit each day.

We're not saying that you have to commit your whole life to school. Just little by little be consistent with your work and understand that you can have an easier life, especially when it comes to school.

C. P. And what makes people – give me some idea – what would make a person stay consistent? Be they young or old, what makes people stay consistent?

L. P. Well, people stay consistent because they choose to stay consistent. We are already consistent in several things.

You consistently get up out of bed at a certain time and get ready for school. That's one type of consistency. You consistently eat dinner at a certain time. That's consistency as well.

Anything you do over the course of a day that repeats over and over at a certain time and at a certain place could be considered consistency.

For example, everyday before bed, I write in my journal, and I write at least maybe a page or two about my thoughts of that day and the thoughts of maybe a few days ago or what my thoughts are now. And I've been doing that consistently because I just chose to.

I chose to not forget every night to do that before I go to bed.

C. P.   So basically, you're saying consistency is a choice?

L. P.   Consistency is a choice because consistency is something you do every single day over the course of the continuous days. Sometimes, we have those days where we get off track. We get off track, and we lose it for maybe one or a few days.

But consistency and persistence go together; you persist to be consistent again.

C. P.   I see.

L. P.   So, maybe you forgot to get up in the morning one day early because your alarm clock didn't wake you up. Well the next day, you don't forget to turn on your alarm, and you wake up the next day on time. That's consistency.

When you miss, you're likely to be more aware the next. You are more aware of your lack of consistency when you miss.

C. P.   So, what can you suggest to help someone who wants to stop procrastinating and who wants to be more consistent? What suggestions could you give?

L. P.   I would say that they need to be a little bit more determined in what they're doing. If they choose to do something, they have to stick with it. There's no going around it.

If they say they want to exercise at 6 o'clock in the morning everyday, they have to consistently get up at that time, and they have to remember. Put it on your calendar. Write it down. Remember.

But consistency and persistence go together; you persist to be consistent again.

However you like planning, you do it like that, and you have to consistently think about it. If you're really determined to do something, it will just happen.

C. P.   Interesting. So basically, if I understand correctly what your perspective is, it is that consistency doesn't just happen by luck, it happens by choice. It's not something that's easy, but it's something that people do if they find that what they need to do is important enough. Would that be correct?

L. P. Yes. People do what they feel is important. Whatever they feel is important, they're very determined to do. And whatever they feel is important, they're going to get it done. Whether it takes a few days a few weeks, or a few months, they're going to get it done.

C. P. So then, why would you say the young person who's having trouble, let's say, studying might want to procrastinate?

L. P. Well, when people are aware that their grades are dropping because they don't understand the subject, they need to step it up and they need to get help to get their grades up.

If the teacher gives you extra credit by giving them special lessons after school or before lunch, you take advantage of all those opportunities. If there's a tutoring program after school or during school, you take those, and you do what it takes to get your results.

Now, you can't get results if you don't make a plan for it. You can't get results if you just don't think about it and do nothing. You have to take action; you have to just go and do it.

C. P. And so, would you – would you say that consistency is difficult for most people?

L. P. Nothing – I'm just going to say this right now – *nothing* is difficult unless you *believe* it's difficult!

C. P. Okay. I can say Amen to that. So then based on that, most people just believe that something is difficult when it really doesn't have to be.

L. P. Yes. Calculus could be difficult to one person while it could be a breeze for somebody else.

C. P. Interesting. Because one person is open to learning and another person is resistant?

L. P. Exactly, one person feels that they can do something because they enjoy it, and the other person feels like it's a bother.

C. P. Interesting.

L. P. You have to have a different way of thinking when you want to get something done. You have to love the subject that you're failing in. You have to love...

C. P. Wait, wait, wait! Hold on. Let's back up. What did you say?

L. P. You have to love the subject that you're failing in.

C. P. You have to *love* the subject that you're failing in. Wow! And how do you do that?

L. P. You just make the choice. It's just that; it's a *choice*. If I tell you to think of a purple elephant, you're going to *automatically* think of a purple elephant.

C. P. Yes.

L. P. You just think about it with no effort.

C. P. Yes, I don't know how to do it. I just choose it?

L. P. You just *choose* to think about a purple elephant.

C. P. So, loving something is as simple as just choosing it?

L. P. Yes. Because think about it, do you excel well in subjects that you hate?

C. P. No, not at all.

L. P. No. You can't excel in the subject that you constantly say that you dislike. You hate the teacher, you hate the class, and you hate the subject or whatever. You can't exceed in a subject that you mentally hate. You just can't.

C. P. Yes, you're right.

L. P. Think about it. When you love a subject, you are more open, and you care about the subject a lot more than if you said you hated it.

C. P. So, the things that would allow a person to stay focused and persist is to remove all negativity toward the thing that they have to do. If you're going to have to do something, it's useless to be negative about it.

L. P. Yes. It's just useless to complain about it. Don't complain about a subject that you're failing in. Don't blame the teacher. You could always get around it. I've been in those situations before where my teacher just did not teach well. I've had teachers who had a poor way of executing lessons. And we just have to get over it.

We have to do whatever it takes to pass those classes. Okay. You know he might be a little bit rude. It doesn't matter. You have to get through it. If you want to get results, you have to get through it all, and you have to get past all the negativity.

And if you can't love the subject at first, just at least pretend for the time being. Just keep repeating in your head, "Oh, I love Math." "I love Science." "I love English." Whatever subject you feel the least confident about, just repeat to yourself that you will exceed in the subject. You love the subject. You enjoy the students. You enjoy the teacher. You enjoy the class.

C. P. Because I think one time you said when we were eating breakfast, you said, "It's okay--sometimes to lie to yourself, as long as it's positive because sooner or later, you'll believe it."

L. P. Yes. It's okay to lie to yourself as long as it's positive, as long as it gets you to do what must be done because sooner or later, you're going to start believing it. Sooner or later, the Math class that you hated is going to be the class that you're exceeding in the most.

C. P. So once you accept it, it's no longer a lie?

L. P. Yes.

C. P. Then it becomes the truth for yourself.

L. P. Yes, exactly. You just have to form your own truths.

C. P. Very interesting. Even if it starts with something that you

would think is not true. It becomes true...

L. P. Exactly.

C. P. Through consistent repetition?

L. P. Yes.

C. P. I see. I see. Okay. That's very interesting. So then in summary, we are saying that consistency is the key to success. Is that what we're saying?

L. P. Yes. Consistency is the key to success, especially if you're being consistent on something that's important to you.

C. P. Because starting and stopping something doesn't get you anywhere, does it?

L. P. No. Starting and stopping doesn't get you anywhere.

C. P. So, there we have it - from my 16-year-old daughter, Luzemily Prosper. And is there anything else you want to say before we wrap it for the day, my baby?

L. P. No, that's about it. We could wrap it up right here.

C. P. Okay everyone, see you next time.

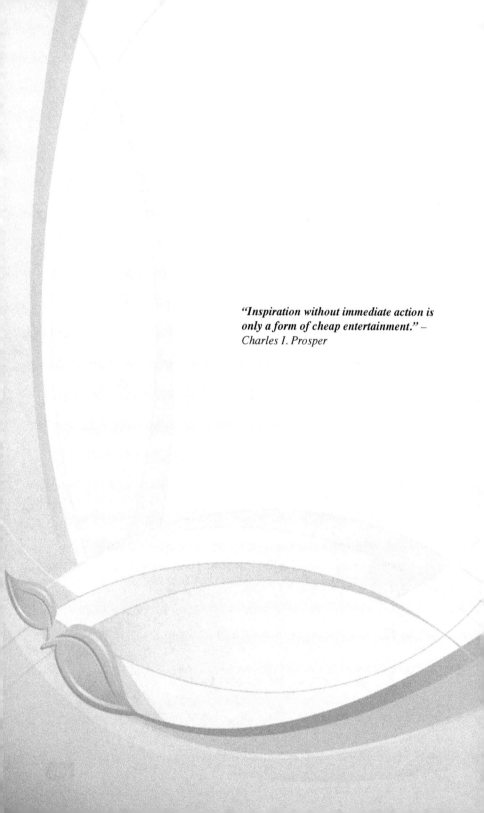

"Inspiration without immediate action is only a form of cheap entertainment." – *Charles I. Prosper*

21

Do Something – Just Don't Skip

Once you have made the commitment to pursue a goal and to remain consistent with the most obvious first steps, there is a great feeling of exhilaration and excitement in feeling the forward motion to success. But life happens. What I mean by this is that you can be on a roll for two or three weeks - or even months of non-stop consistent practice when suddenly there is an impasse. Something gets in the way of the full completion of your activity. Let us say that you have been making it to the gym every morning for 40 days; your car won't start. If you catch a bus to the gym, you will lose 30 minutes of workout time. So, what do you do? Instead of your usual 60-minute workout, you can only do half. What would *you* normally do in a situation like this? Would you just accept the unkind fate for the day, and wait until tomorrow to "make up for lost time?" Or would you catch the bus, make it to the gym, and put in the 30 minutes that you can do? I would submit to you that "something" always registers on the plus sign of the ledger while "doing nothing" is not the same as standing still. Doing nothing is always a step backwards, because life never stands still; it is either moving forward or traveling backwards. Even though you may not *perceive* that skipping once is equivalent to moving backwards, but it becomes progressively more evident, the more you skip. The more you skip, the more likely you will tend to continue to skip, until consistency has been completely undermined.

Consistency Does Not Have to Be All or Nothing

All or nothing is the mantra of the perfectionist, and in my opinion, perfectionists are among some of the biggest non-acheivers in the world. Perfectionists don't get things done because they are lost in the illusion of their perfection. To wait until something is "perfect," before taking action, provides a convenient justification for procrastination. I even remember reading somewhere a quote that humorously makes my point. "Anything worth doing is worth doing *lousy!* Just do something – *anything!* Make corrections later!"

When you catch your vision and have the "fire in your belly" to move, you must move *quickly.* You cannot allow yourself to be impeded by the paralysis of analysis. The Bible puts it this way, "Write the vision; make it plain on tablets, so he may run who reads it." – Habakkuk 2:2. Make note that it doesn't say "so he may *walk* who reads it," or, "so he may *stroll* who reads it." It clearly says that you must act quickly and run, run, *run* with your vision! Don't think too much about it. Just act on it! Run for your life!

It's Not Always What You Do – But Only That You Do

I, for several months now, have gotten up at 4:20 a.m. to write for at least one hour in this book, the book you are holding in your hands right now. Sometimes, I get up at 3:30 a.m., and I write a little more. One thing is for sure, there are those days that I definitely want to just stay in bed, get more sleep, and tell myself that it's okay to skip for just today – but somehow, I don't. Discipline and determination is not for the faint of heart. I can understand why most people just won't do it. I can also understand why super-achievers will always remain in the minority. There are times when, for practical reasons, I can't do a full hour or more of writing. Just the other day, I was under the weather, coughing, sneezing, stuffy nose, the whole nine yards. I slept until 7:30 a.m., several hours later than my usual starting time, yet I got up and wrote for 15 minutes. Was writing 15 minutes instead of an hour significant? I'll say it was! I was able to manage my morning rhythm, though less, by maintaining an unboken thread of consistency. It took me three days to recover from my illness. The second day, I wrote for 30 minutes. The third day, I wrote for 45 minutes, and by the fourth day, I was back to my minimum one-hour a day schedule. Former President Theodore Roosevelt had it right when he said, "Do what you can, with what you have, where you are."

Though I digress, this timely wisdom is also an elegant argument *against* the strict adherence to popular "success-formulas" promulgated by today's on-stage personal motivators and success gurus. When we look and attempt to follow a success formula, no matter how exciting it sounds, we are not primarily looking at where *we* are; we are looking at where the success guru *was*, when he or she started, and then we try to *force* ourselves into their past life situation as though it were our own.

What we have and what we can do is *always* going to be different from the situation of someone else's. Everyone's life situation is like a fingerprint, unique, different, and special, one that will always require a custom-made solution. Solutions come, but they come in the process of doing – doing what you must do, that is, what is most obvious to do according to your current life situation.

The Temptation to Skip Will Always Rear Its Ugly Head

As I have stressed througout all of this book is that consistency doesn't happen by default. What this means is that the activities and influences of your life situation and environment may not be on the same page with your goals. You may wake up at 4:00 a.m. to go to the gym and workout for an hour, but your daughter may have gotten up feeling ill, thus necessitating that you go over to the drugstore to get her a remedy. You may have to take off a few days from work, for whatever reason; this means that you won't be able to save up your target $500 for this month. To all unavoidable and unexpected life situations, I say do what you can with the time or resources that you have. If possible, don't skip.

As a couple of practical examples, if you don't have the time to do 100 sit-ups today – do 20, but just don't skip. If you are unable to save $500 this month, if you can, save $250 – just don't skip saving for the month.

Skipping Always Leads to Quitting

Skipping and quitting are connected on an unseen continuum that begins with the first time you skip. Skipping once is your first step toward quitting. Practice always leads to improvement. Your psycho-biological organism is goal-oriented and interprets all repeated activity as a goal that has been ordained by you. So, whatever you begin to do and continue to do repeatedly, your psycho-biological organism takes over and "helps" you by making you feel more "in the mood" to do that repeated activity easier and better the next. This psycho-servo-mechanism is fine as long as the goal positive and self-fulfilling, but it become a double-edged sword if, consciously or unconsciouly, you direct it to a habit that will lead you *away* from positive results and self-fullment.

To exercise or not exercise, to practice or not practice, that is the question. The answer is when it comes to your important and firmly established goals, imperfect practice is better than none at all.

Moods Are Not Your Friend

What is a mood? A mood is an internal mental climate, which can result from a multitude of known or unknown emotional factors, which can temporarily impact the psychological state of an individual.

There is a field of study called biorhythms, which says that all humans have three basic cycles of energy fluctuation: a physical cycle, which is said to be every 23 days, an emotional cycle, which is said to go up and down every 28 days, and an intellectual cycle, which is said to last every 33 days.

If you live long enough, you will realize that you have "high days" and "low days." A mood may be influenced by known or unknown biorhythms of an individual.

There have been anecdotal and historical correlates to the lunar influence on emotional states. The term "lunatic," which means "one who is affected by the moon" has been known throughout the ages and in many cultures of the world. In Spanish, we say "lunático," which again reflects the erratic behavior of an individual during a full moon cycle.

The tides are periodic rises and falls of large bodies of water, such as the ocean. The gravitational pull of the full moon on the Earth causes the waters of the ocean to bulge in the direction of the moon's pull, thus the resulting in a tidal wave. The human body, in a healthy adult, is made up of about 75% water. Thus, if the full moon is strong enough to pull the waters of the ocean, there is no reason to believe that it could not also be strong enough to "pull" the waters of our bodies in such a way to possibly to cause some sort of temporary emotional imbalance, better known as a "bad" mood.

A person can have a bad dream that leaves negative emotional residue in the mind upon awakening, yet many times the details of dream may have been forgotten, however the emotional feeling residue still remains in the form of a mood. The sooner you realize that a mood wants to take over, the better off you will be.

If you detect a mood, and allow it to take its course, you will find that it has a mind of its own. It can and will influence you accordingly – *if* you do not take *immediate* control! Unwittingly, moods get their authority and their power to take over *from you!* It is imperative stand up, confront, and immediately take charge of your mind.

You can change your mood, but you must do it *quickly* – *as soon* as you notice it. You must nip it in the bud, for if you wait too long, it takes over, and it takes control. The key to remember is that your mood *will* do what you conscious mind tells it to do.

Tell Your Thoughts What to Think

I remember a technique that I learned from one of my spiritual teachers, the late and controversial mind science minister, Rev. Ike. I remember a sermon that he gave on controlling unwanted thoughts, the kind of thoughts that tell you that you don't feel like what you are supposed to being doing. Here, you must tell your thoughts what to think.

The key to the success of this technique is to nip these thoughts in the bud. What this means is that you only have a 30-second window to take action. Once a negative thought has gained some momentum, it will call forth additional negative thoughts to reinforce it and assist in the assault. Beyond a certain point, it is very, very difficult to reverse negative thinking that has taken control.

I like to give this metaphoric example. Let us say that a person is smoking a cigarette, and a small piece of burning ash falls on the top of your pants leg. If you *quickly* brush the burning ash aside and off of your pants, there will be little or no damage to the fabric. However, if you hesitate and allow the burning ash to take hold, it is likely that it will burn a hole in the fabric of your pants causing irreparable damage along with scorching the skin of your thigh. As soon as you detect a negative thought or mood, *speak* directly to it and *out loud* as though it were a conscious entity, which, parenthetically, it *is*. "Listen to me! I am in control today. There will be none of this laziness and lethargy. I feel good! I feel great! I feel terrific! I can do this!" As hackneyed as the idea of self-pep talk appears to be, it does have one distinct advantage – it works! Do this for 10 to 15 minutes, and you will notice that you have shifted your mood from negative to positive.

Tell Your Feelings How to Feel

By default, when you tell your thoughts what to think, you are telling your feelings how to feel. We feel *as* we think. Conscious-control thinking is something that must be practiced and exercised regularly in the same way that we would exercise a muscle. The forebrain, the thinking part of the brain, the cerebral cortex, will develop new pathways and complex neuronal connections, a term scientist call "neural plasticity." The more you practice conscious-control thinking, the better you will get at it, and this "thinking muscle" will develop accordingly.

You can tell your feelings how to feel by addressing them directly as though they were an entity, over which you have the power to order and to control. "Feelings! Listen to me! I am in control today. There will be none of this laziness and lethargy. I feel good! I feel great! I feel terrific!

Eventually, you get to the point where you can change from a way you feel now to the way you want to feel – but it takes practice. With consistent practice, you will succeed, and you will learn to tell your thoughts what to think and your feelings how to feel.

"I am at the stage of my life where I know that the majority of people will never do what the minority of successful people are always willing to do." – Charles I. Prosper

The "Average" Person Is Not Consistent

After being on this Earth for more than half a century, I have come to the conclusion that, when it comes to achieving great success in life, there are basically two categories of people: the average and the above average. In most psychological literature, whenever you see the term average person, you see "average" in quotation marks. The reason for the quotation marks is that *average* must be defined and not assumed. I would say that for me average is someone who belongs to the vast majority of the total population. Percentage-wise, the average person, by my estimation, belongs to about 90% of any population sample of a few thousand people or more. The larger the population sample, the more accurate the picture of the shared beliefs and behaviors.

The Average Person Follows the Crowd

When it comes to being mediocre, majority always rules. Most people want to belong, not make waves, not be iconoclastic, or rock the boat. Most people don't set high goals, and most people don't consistently follow through on their goals by taking any regular daily action. As harsh as it sounds, most people are supposed to be average, otherwise "above-average" could not even be possible.

We live in a world pyramid of strata-achievement. The majority of people *choose* to stay near the middle or at the bottom of the population pyramid. As we gradually move toward the top, toward the upper layers of the population pyramid, we notice that it begins to narrow, where we begin to find a different caliber-mindset of people. These are people who *regularly* set goals, make plans of action, and are willing to do whatever it takes. These are people who take calculated and intelligent risks. These are people who don't talk about what they are going to do to everyone before they do it; these are people who quietly and confidently take action and make their dreams come true.

If we continue to the peak of the population pyramid, we notice that it's not crowded at the top; the air is cleaner, and the view is expansive and more beautiful. There is more vision at the top. At the top, things can be seen which hardly could be even imagined toward the bottom.

My 16-year-old daughter, Luzemily related to me an interesting incident during her high school World History class. The subject was on world poverty. The professor was trying to make a case for justifying poverty.

"So, Luzemily, what do you think about poverty and the poor?" asks the teacher.

She answered, "People cannot avoid being *born* poor, but most people *stay* poor by the *choices* they make thereafter." This brought the house down! My daughter came under the virulent attack of the "majority" of the class. The majority of the class identified themselves as "poor" or disadvantaged, proudly raising their "banners of victimology."

The "Bell Shaped" Curve of Populations Statistics
In the study of psychology and statistics there is a graph which shows the distribution of achievement, intelligence, and performance of any large population sample of several

thousand people or more. This distribution graph is called the Bell Shape Curve. For example, IQ (Intelligence Quotient), by whatever standard it is chosen to be measured, conforms to the Bell Shape Curve. Look at the example below.

Bell Shaped Curve Ilustration

If you notice the drawing on the napkin, you will see two arrows. The horizontal arrow on the bottom, that moves from left to right, represents, if we are talking about IQ, the two extremes of mental capacity. The extreme left represents those who are mentally challenged; the extreme right represents those who are considered "gifted" or highly intelligent. The middle represents where most or the majority of people lie, thus the term "average."

The vertical arrow represents the percentage of the total population. The population percentage is lowest at the two opposite extremes; the majority of the people, the average individual, forms the greatest aggregation, where the vertical arrow runs from the bottom to the top, at the middle.

IQ is not the only human attribute that conforms to the bell shaped curve. Most human behavior conforms to the bell shaped curve. When it comes to positive human characteristics, the bell shaped curve is a result of how the majority versus the minority make choices.

How many people on January 1st, set New Year's resolutions? Check with those same people in July or August of the same year, and you will find that the total population of people who have kept their New Year's resolutions will conform to the bell shaped curve. The majority of the people will have given up. As the bell slopes downward to each side, the left side represents the percentage of those who didn't bother to make any New Year's Resolution, and as the bell slopes downward on the right side, this represents the small percentage of people who kept up their New Year's until and throughout July and August.

If 3000 people attend a Tony Robbins how-to-get-rich motivation workshop, my belief and experience is that if you follow the progress of all 3000 people who left this workshop highly motivated, over the course of several months, you will again see the bell shaped curve of achievement. Only a small percentage, maybe 5 or 10% of the total attendees will have followed through and have consistently taken action; *most* will have gone back to their former daily routines.

Let's not stop here. How about the people who say they want to enroll in a gym and lose weight? The majority of people will start, and after a certain period of time, will fall off and stop going. Only the *minority* will remain consistent, thus again we will see the bell shaped curve. I would be bold enough to say that consistency conforms to a bell shaped curve whenever the vast majority of population attempt to achieve *any* significant goal.

People have asked me to give them the "secret" of writing and publishing a book. I say that there is no secret to writing a book. It is just a matter of consistency. Then some will say, "But I work for full-time how can find time to do this? I reply, "No problem. Just go to bed by 8:30 p.m., and wake up by 4:30 AM, and write an hour every day, accomplishing a page a day, and within six months anyone can write a book of at least 180 pages. Now I ask you, how many people do you think will be willing to do this? Do you think that the *majority* will be willing to do this? So, do you see my point?

There has never been a time in the history of the human race, even if we go back centuries or eons, where the *minority* has not always stood out and has achieved the most. Don't get mad with me, I didn't set it up this way. I was born into a world like this. This is the way it has always been, and I dare say that this is that way it will *always* be.

Even the Bible (John 12:8) says, "The poor will always be amongst us." And I say that *you* don't have to be one of them! It's your *choice* to be prosperous. Will you take this choice? Most people don't. It's just the way it is. Don't look at the way the world usually chooses. Just look in the mirror. Who you see in the mirror is the answer. How do *you* choose?

Motivational speakers naively believe or want to believe that they can motivate you and others to be successful. This belief can also said to be true of most therapists, many teachers, and a lot of social workers, those who believe that they can motivate people to change.

My good friend, Joseph Daniel, once told me, "The surfer cannot create the wave – he can only *ride* it!" Likewise, I say that no person, audio, or book *(not even mine!)* can create light. The only thing that a "motivator" or teacher can do is to be the bellow that blows the spark in the people. The person must come with a spark already lit. We therefore can blow the spark of another to help that spark glow hot, but we do not *create* the spark. The spark of change comes from God. We, as teachers, are only *facilitators* of that spark.

Metaphorically, if I go to the supermarket aisle and look for the shelf where the bags of charcoal are being sold, I can rip open a bag, take out my bellows and blow on the bag of charcoal non-stop, and there will be no light. If the spark is not already there, I am only blowing air upon dead coals.

So, it is with people who are ready to change, once God touches us with the spark of enlightenment, the student is ready, and the teacher will appear. Isn't curious that we rarely hear anyone say, "The guru enlightened him," rather, we hear, "He was enlightened, or he became enlightened."

When speaking of Teaching, Kahil Gibran, in *The Prophet*, succintly tells us, "No man can reveal to you aught but that which already lies half asleep in the dawning of your knowledge."

Most People Are Supposed to Be Average

The Bible says (Matthew 5:5), "The meek will inherit the Earth." The "meek" *(insert average people)* will "inherit" *(insert overpopulate)* the Earth. Prosper's translation is "Average people will overpopulate the Earth." Most people are supposed to be average; otherwise, how could above-average even exist? This is a reality that may be a little hard to swallow, especially if you consider *yourself* as average, but this is the way the world is set up. At 11-years-old, my daughter, Luzemily said, "If everyone was a millionaire then no one would be a millionaire," page 75, *The Sayings of Luzemily, The 7-Year-Old Sage*.

We live in a world of a population-pyramid. A top could not exist were there not a bottom or middle strata. *Where* you ultimately find yourself on the world population-pyramid, I say, is primarily a matter of *choice*. If you do not believe then it is a matter of choice, then you have unwittingly chosen where you are destined to be. Most people ignore their power to choose. Choice is a power, a right, a privilege, and an obligation. "Choose you this day whom you will serve," (Joshua 24:15). Do you choose this day success? Or do you choose this day failure? Even a failure to make a conscious choice is *still* a choice, by default. You get the luck of the draw.

Everyday is "this day." You must choose *every* day whom you will serve. You cannot choose yesterday. You can only choose *this day*. You cannot choose tomorrow. You can only choose *this day*. Choosing each and every day whom you will serve is what consistency is all about.

Consistency doesn't happen by default. It is a choice. For it to happen automatically and without your decision would be a violation of your free will. Because consistency involves discipline and sacrifice, it is contrary to human nature. "Human nature" always seeks the path of least resistance, but it is by choosing the road less traveled by that the rewards of this life are ultimately found.

"God wants you to succeed to the degree that you are willing to do whatever it takes to succeed." – Charles I. Prosper

Consistency is the Envelope of Success Principles

In February of 2015, I published an incredible book entitled *The 12 Laws of Success* (available on Amazon.com and BarnesandNoble.com). Of course I'm a little biased because I wrote the book, nevertheless, this book has served as the text for many Success Focus Groups and workshops that I have offered in Southern California, that have helped and guided many people. In this chapter, I would like to go over what those 12 laws of success entail, and then introduce the premise that no law or principle of success is worth anything until and unless it is coupled with the principle of consistency. Consistency is the envelope of the 12 laws of success.

The 12 Laws of Success

So, before I explain how the 12 laws of success relate to consistency, let us take a quick look at what each of these laws entail:

Law #1 - Goal Setting

Law #2 - Belief

Law #3 - Positive Expectation

Law #4 - Detachment

Law #5 - Attraction

Law #6 - Planning

Law #7 - Willingness

Law #8 - Immediate Action

Law #9 - Persistence

Law #10 - Financial Planning

Law #11 - Gratitude

Law #12 - Giving

Law # 1 - Goal Setting

The first law of success is the law of goal setting. Goal setting involves our power to choose. Where you go in life will not be ordained by anyone but will be chosen by you. Your parents cannot choose your goals. Your teacher cannot choose your goals. Your spouse cannot choose your goals. Even God will not choose your goals, for this would be a violation of your free will, which can never be taken away from you.

A man without a goal is like a ship without a rudder. If you got into a motor boat, which had no rudder, rebbed it up and let it go out into the ocean without any control or guiding force, it would be very easy to imagine that this boat would soon crash into a rock , another boat, and capsize to the ocean floor. This is exactly what we do when we go along day-by-day just *hoping* that something better will happened to us or at least nothing worse than we are currently experiencing. This is living by default. Even making no choice is still a choice – a choice to go nowhere.

How Consistency Relates to Goal Setting

There are people who set a goal, come across an obstacle or set-back, drop the original goal, and then jump to something else. The second "goal" is initiated, and everything goes fine. There is an unexpected challenge, so what is it that they do? They drop this second goal, and try something new. If not checked, this becomes a pernicious pattern of jumping from one thing to the next without staying with any one thing long enough to see any fruit. This is where persistence comes in. If the goal is worthy of accomplishment, it is worthy of your persistence, Persistence is the motor which moves consistency. Without consistency, your goal cannot move forward and survive.

Law # 2 - Belief

The second law of success is the law of belief. Once you decide upon a goal, what determines if you will persist or not is the belief in yourself and the possibility of achieving your objective. What exactly is a belief? A belief is a feeling of certainty about a certain experience, idea, situation, or observation. Your beliefs not only determine what choices you make and what you do, your beliefs also determine how your body will respond. It would be correct to say that our life experience is nothing but a well-organized belief system wrought and molded consciously or unconsciously by our own devices. Napoleon Hill in his classic book, *Think and Grow Rich,* pronounced these words that continue to echo through the halls of self-improvement and self-realization, "Anything that the mind of man can conceive and believe can be achieved." And how are beliefs formed when they are consciously intended? Simply by repetition, and stating "I believe...such-and-such," and then immediately acting on it with confidence and certainty.

How Consistency Relates to Belief

Part of this question was answered in the previous section when I say that a belief is consciously formed by repetition and immediately acting on it. The process of repetition and acting on a newly chosen belief will not produce fruit overnight. It is usually a matter of consistently believing and acting such that your action conforms with the belief. In time, and with patience, a new belief system formed, and then your mind takes over and it becomes *automatically* who you are. You have become the belief and the belief has become you.

Law # 3 - Positive Expectation

The third law of success is the law of positive expectation. You might say that positive expectation is a type of belief, but we are also talking about a very powerful and creative use of the mind. It is a type of mental climate, or positive attitude, as it were, of faith that Life is good and that Life loves you. This requires, for some, a entire reshifting of philosophical assumptions about Life and how we relate to "God."

What you expect, you get. When you expect the best, I believe that you release a powerful and magnetic force for good. This powerful and magnetic force becomes what some call the Law of Attraction, which we'll cover in Law #5. If you expect the worst to happen, somehow the worst usually befalls you. "For the thing which I greatly feared is come upon me," (The Bible, Job 3:25). If you expect the best and trust in the bounty of Life, you will be led to the ways and means of creating the best ways to rapidly create what you desire. Positive attitude and sustained faithful expectancy is the key. The person who expects to grow old at 70, usually does so, and the person who expects to grow stronger and healthier with each passing year, greatly retards the aging process by looking and feeling much younger than whatever chronological age that he or she has reached.

How Consistency Relates to Positive Expectation

Positive expectation lies on a continuum from beginning to completion of the desired objective. You cannot positively expect one moment, and start doubting the next. This on-off switching would cancel the effect. To sustain yourself in a state of positive expectation, it must be done persistently, faithfully, and consistently. If you expect to be lucky, you will be lucky.

Law # 4 - Detachment

The fourth law of success is the law of detachment. Detachment is another way of saying trust, and the mechanism by which detachment operates is patience. The best example that I can give of detachment is when you plant a seed in fertile ground. Beyond your responsibility of watering the soil and making sure that it stays fertile, you can do no more that wait, become patient, and *detach*. The 12 laws are not discreet but are interconnected with each other in the same way that a rainbow is formed by a continuum of color, which blends together from red, to orange, to yellow, to green, to blue, and to purple, making it is difficult to tell exactly where one color begins and another one ends. The law of detachment is predicated on the belief that a seed will spout with the positive expectation that, in the end, all will go well.

Detachment means, in essence, that you do your thing and you let God do His. Your job is to chose what you want, intend to have it, take action, and observe the results. If something works, do more of it; if something doesn't work, do less of it. You see, this taking-action and observation-of-results is your spiritual dialogue between you and Higher Power. If you get caught up with the worry of why something doesn't work out exactly as you planned, you become attached to a specific result instead of detaching and enjoying the experience of your personal and spiritual evolution. Detachment, acceptance, and patience always leads to peace, spiritual growth and success.

WHY CONSISTENCY IS KEY TO ALL SUCCESS

How Consistency Relates to Detachment

Detachment only works when it is coupled with patience, and patience can only show its true power over time. Consistently remaining patient is essentially the practice of daily detachment. If you detach today, it is by choice, and therefore, tomorrow you must do the same. You plant. You pray. You wait. And in time, you will see the results of your planned persistence and patience.

Law # 5 - Attraction (Opportunity)

The fifth law of success is the law of attraction. Much to-do and misconception surround this law. It is thought by many people that this law works when you focus on something intently, you automatically become attracted to it. Well, yes and no. It also matters *how* you focus on something. As when have already mentioned, it is important that you firmly believe in the object of your focus, and assuming it is a goal, your focus should be infused with positive expectation and supported by a detached state of mind.

There is something else that I want to clarify about this so-called Law of Attraction. The Law of Attraction is a misnomer. This is really The Law of Opportunity. I believe that our inner guidance system consciously or unconsciously leads us to the ideal circumstances or to the key people that will make the realization of our goal possible. However, we are still obligated to *act* on the opportunities that we have been attracted to. If I want to meet the woman of my dreams, and I see someone who catches my eye at work or at a social event, I still have the obligation to take action, walk up to her, and ask her out for a date. If I want to get into physical shape, and I suddenly discover a new gym that is opening up only walking distance from my home, I still have to take action on this opportunity by enrolling and starting to exercise. The Law of Attraction, or as I like to put it, The Law of Opportunity is connected to Law # 8, The Law of Immediate Action, which we will cover a little later.

How Consistency Relates to Attraction (Opportunity)

Attracting opportunity into your experience serves absolutely no purpose is you are not *consistently* taking action on each and every opportunity that is presented to you. I do not believe that opportunity knocks only once, but I do believe that each opportunity is unique and will never repeat itself *exactly* the same way in the future. So, it behooves you to *repeatedly* take advantage of *every* opportunity, and not just once in a while.

Law # 6 - Planning

The sixth law of success is the law of planning. You start with a goal, then follows a plan, which delineates the details of what you intend to do. However, this is the secret to planning: A plan is not fixed and set in stone, especially in the beginning. It is only the springboard. A plan is a living and breathing organism, which expands and contracts according to the needs and changes of your progress. A plan evolves as you do, and grows and changes as you do. What you need to know and what you need to do now will be different from what you need to know and do later. With growth comes a *change* in your plans. Your goals and plans at 20 are probably not going to be the same goals and plans at age 60.

How Consistency Relates to Planning

Because your planning must evolve and grow as your situation changes, there must be a consistent awareness and willingness to improve and modify your path as you go. So, I am saying that with every plan you make for any goal that you set, there must be the Overall Plan to change, improve, and modify what you must do as you continue to move forward in progress.

Law # 7 - Willingness

The seventh law of success is the law of willingness to do whatever it takes. This law #7 of willingness makes all of the other laws possible. Without a willingness to do whatever it takes, you would not choose to believe, to have positive expectancy, to detach when necessary, or to act when opportunity presents itself. Willingness is the right attitude and the right mental posture, but the litmus test always happens in the moment that you take action. Taking action is the *validation* of your willingness. Willingness is the opening of your heart and the surrender to whatever must be done. There is no resistance. There is total acceptance. There is detachment from any thoughts of the way things *should* be or *supposed* to be.

Willingness to do whatever it takes triggers your intuition. In my own life experience, once I am 100% committed to something happening, which is to say that once I am willing to do whatever is necessary, I have noticed that more intutitive hunches, and more meaningful "coincidences" begin to occur. Intuition is that inner voice of "knowingness." It is when we have a "gut feeling" about (this or that). We are born with this innate servo-mechanism, which I call the voice-of-God within. Willingness triggers the positive flow of Life in *your* direction.

How Consistency Relates to Willingness

Willingness is ongoing and continuous. It is a commitment to *stay* open and ready to act on the guidance that is felt within. I can *predict* the success of someone who is *willing today*, right after attending a motivation seminar, but is *unwilling tomorrow* after the fanfare and the fire has died down. Commitment and willingess go hand in hand. Commitment is the fuel of persistence. The more willing you are and the more committed you are, the wheel of success will revolve faster and faster toward your goal.

Law # 8 - Immediate Action

The eighth law of success is the law of immediate action. I am sure that you have heard the expression, "Strike while the iron is hot." When iron is white hot, it is soft and malleable. If you wait to strike it when it has cooled off, it will again be too hard to shape. So, it is when Opportunity presents itself through the workings of the Law of Attraction. Opportunities not quickly and courageously acted upon become your rationalizations, remorse, and regret thereafter.

The Universe rewards action. The Universe rewards action with results. The Universe rewards immediate action with immediate results. Inspiration is time sensitive. How many times have you had a great idea for a business, a book, or a special project, only to put it off and let it cool off in your mind. Sometimes you find that someone else has taken "your" idea and has run with it. When you are inspired by a great idea, your energy and your motivation is greatest *in the moment* when you first receive it. Providing you don't go around telling everyone and asking for opinions, there is energy and excitement that will build up inside of you creating a pressure from within to take action. It is precisely at the moment of inspration that immediate action is the *most productive.* Action creates more action because the more you do *immediately*, the *faster* you will discover what you will have to do *next.*

How Consistency Relates to Immediate Action

There must be consistent momentum toward your goal. When it is time to take action, you must act quickly to create and keep the momentum going in a positive direction. The actions that you take will either bring you closer or further away from your goal. The secret is quite simple. Whatever you do that brings you closer to your goal, do more of it. Whatever takes you farther from your goal, do less of it. When things are becoming easier and easier, you are on the right track. When things are becoming more and more difficult, you are on the wrong track. "Right" or "wrong" is characterized by the presence or the absence of a feeling-of-peace. If what you are doing brings you a feeling of peace, you are on the right track. If what you are doing makes you "think too much," analyze, compare, cogitate, and worry, you are on the wrong track.

Law # 9 - Persistence

The ninth law of success is the law of persistence. Persistence and consistency go hand in hand. Though similar, they are not the same. Consistency is doing a certain thing in a certain way everyday. Persistence is the *vehicle*, which moves consistency from one point to the next. Success is a gold coin with Consistency on one side and Persistence on the other.

Persistence is that quality which knows that problems are a part of progress. The more difficult the struggle, the sweeter the victory. Persistence is also that quality which is ready, willing, and able to *accept* stumbling blocks, not as problems but as *creative growth opportunities* in the same way that an athlete faces and overcomes challenges and obstacles, which must come *before* every ultimate victory.

The way we see the problem *is* the real problem. Before you call situation a "problem," ask yourself, "What does this mean?" How you answer this question will determine your experience of the situation and your probability of successfully solving it. You can increase your persistence-power by simply choosing to relabel the antiquated term *problem*. Here are some alternative labels, which might serve you instead of using the word *problem*: challenge, situation, growth opportunity, awakening, reality check, wake up call, divine message, or call for creativity. The positive possibilities are virtually endless. Why limit yourself with the overused, hackneyed, and traditionally negative connotations of the word *problem?*

How Consistency Relates to Persistence

Consistency relates to persistence more than any of the other 12 laws because the continued existence of consistency is predicated on persistence to keep it going. Persistence is continuous choice of positive action until the desired outcome happens. From where you are now to where you want to be is no more than the timely crossing-over-the-bridge of problems, however you want to define *problem*. The only thing standing in your way of crossing over to the side of victory is your willingness to take yet *another step forward*. Another step forward, no matter what, can only happen through persistence day in and day out.

Law # 10 - Financial Planning

The tenth law of success is the law of financial planning. Unless you inherit it, wealth does not come by default. Wealth and economic solvency comes through prudent saving and careful financial planning. The subject of financial planning touches upon the understanding of money, i.e., what money is, and how to attract, have and enjoy more of it in your life. I have discovered that there are 7 laws of money, which are:

- 1) *The Law of Saving Money* – Wealth cannot be accumulated unless one saves a percentage of total earnings, usually 10% or more, until enough capital has been saved for investment and increase.

- 2) *The Law of Control of Money* – We live in a consumer society, which tells us that it is better to spend for pleasure and comfort than to save for financial freedom from worry and insecurity. The control of money really is about the control of yourself.

- 3) *The Law of Pay Yourself First (Automatically)* –
  If you work for any large organization and receive a
  paycheck, you will notice that there are various
  deductions which are automatically taken from your
  paycheck when you receive it. Large government
  entities, such as the Internal Revenue Service and
  your State Tax agencies have learned that the best
  way to get paid what they want from you is to deduct
  it *automatically*. This same principle I suggest to you.
  Set up an automatic savings deduction from your
  paycheck that goes directly to a savings that you will
  designate as your long term investment capital sav-
  savings. It is also smart to set up a "bodyguard
  savings" in addition to your capital savings; if a
  money emergency happens, you would need never
  dip into your investment capital savings.

- 4) *The Law of Enjoying Money* – You must enjoy money to increase it. Making money is not just about
  saving money; it is also about enjoying a part of the
  money you earn. This is the spiritual law of attraction. Whatever you enjoy and love, you attract more
  of it into your life. Just as whatever you fear, you
  attract more of it into you life. Every payday, make
  sure you use a portion of your money, after your
  savings and before paying out all of your bills and
  just enjoy it, if it is no more than buying a frozen
  yogurt and enjoying it with your daughter, or taking a
  long trolley ride and enjoy it will all of your heart and
  soul. Do this, and you will attract more money to you.

- 5) *The Law of Giving Money* – Give some of your money
  to help improve the quality of life of others, and your
  money will increase. Arnold Schwarzenegger lists in his

secrets of success that secret #6 is "Give Something Back."

- 6) *The Law of Investing Money* – No one every became wealthy by working a 9 to 5 job. If you want wealth, if you believe in wealth, if feel that you and your family deserve wealth, you must invest your money to increase it. (Parenthetically, still one of the best ways to do this is through real estate.)

- 7) *The Law of Gratitude for Money* – This law of money is related to *The Law of Enjoying Money.* To the degree that you are grateful for money, you will enjoy it more.

How Consistency Relates to Financial Planning

This is probably one of the easiest to see. The essence of successful financial planning *is* consistency. For example, successful retirement planning assumes consistency. If you consult with any experienced financial planner, he or she will usually talk about having a regular savings, one which earns a certain high interest rate, and increases your money, which you don't touch of course, over an extended period of, say, 10, 20, or 30 years. Starting at 25-years-old, with a good retirement savings plans, most people could retire by age 50. The only caveat of all good retirement savings plans is that most people don't save successfully because saving requires consistency.

Law # 11 - Gratitude

The eleventh law of success is the law of gratitude. However you define success, if happiness is not a main component of your success, I find that it is a very shallow accomplishment. The Law of Gratitude is the law of happiness. There is always an immediate reward for gratitude, and that is joy. If anyone wants a quick and guaranteed recipe for happiness, I would say, count your blessings. This is not a new idea. Some might even say that it is just common sense, but again, how *common* is "common" sense. I recommend that practicing gratitude become a regular daily practice, where you set aside at least 15 minutes in the morning and/or at least 15 minutes in the evening, before bedtime, and recognize or count your blessings one by one. No matter what your religious orientation or how you define it, gratitude is prayer. Bless all that is beautiful and wonderful, large and small, in your life. Bless you and thank you are synonymous. I believe that a grateful heart brings you closer to the bosom of God and the continued blessings of God. I believe that God hears best from those whose lips come the words that are carried by wings of gratefulness.

How Consistency Relates to Gratitude

The key to all positive principles is that, for them to work, they must become a way of life. Should you be grateful today, and hateful the tomorrow? Of course not. You would choose this today and each day which quality or trait to serve. For gratitude to have its full effect, must be *practiced* - and you guessed it - *consistently!*

Law # 12 - Giving

The twelfth law of success is the law of giving. Giving is such a spiritual and personal principle that there is no way to prove the positive effect that it will have on your life until you give it a try and practice it for any length of time. No matter what you might expect to receive from giving, one thing is for sure, giving from the heart will always result in an immediate sense of peace - a peace the surpasses all understanding. Even if you do not believe in "God," when you give of yourself with the intention to improve the quality of life of others in any way or on any level, the reward will always be a sense peace, joy, or love. On Giving, Kahil Gibran, in *The Prophet* says, "And is there aught you would withhold? All you have shall some day be given; Therefore give now, that the season of giving may be yours and not your inheritors."

How Consistency Relates to Giving

Just like the principle of gratitude, the full effect and experience of giving can only be felt once giving has become a natural and integral part of who you are. As paradoxical as it may sound, sharing is having more. I like the way my teacher, Rev Ike, used to say it, "God gives to the giver, and takes from the taker."

*"Consistency + patience = persistence.
Persistence = success."* – Charles I. Prosper

24

When Does Consistency End?

The flow of Life will never stop. Life is always moving, changing, pulsating, and renewing. Consistency is inevitable because Life must consistently move either up or down, in or out, front or back. You will either progress by choice or digress by default. What I have been saying all throughout this book is that consistency is a choice, and it is a choice that must be made again and again each day. The fact of life is that the majority of people *choose* not to consistent and do the things that they say are important to them. I can't change that. This is the way it is, and this is the way it has always been throughout human history, and I dare say that this is the way it will *always* be. However, my message is that *you* do not have to be one who chooses not to be consistent. *You* do not have to be among the majority who choose not consistency. You can choose to be consistent, and you can choose to do so – starting right now.

The Consistency Prayer

"Dear God, let me be more consistent in my life." – Joseph Daniel.

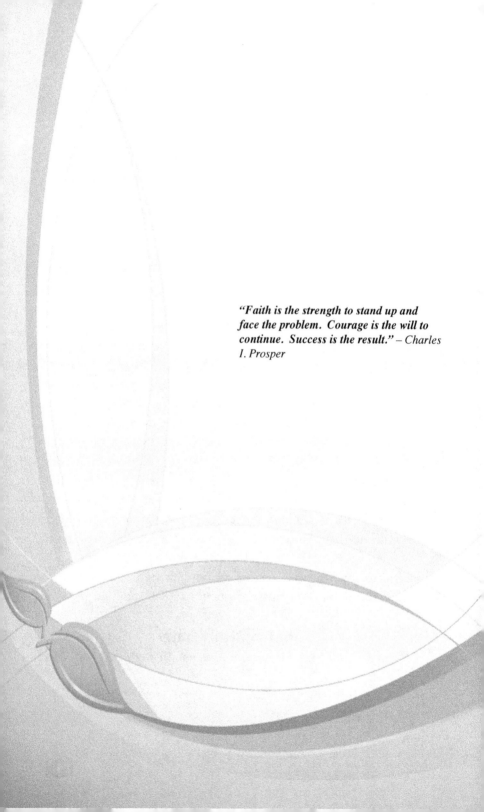

"Faith is the strength to stand up and face the problem. Courage is the will to continue. Success is the result." – *Charles I. Prosper*

Selected Resources

Aikido in Daily Life, Koichi Tohei. ISBN 978-0870402210

Biography.com

207 Inspirational Quotes of Charles I. Prosper, Charles I. Prosper. ISBN 978-0-943845-22-7

The 12 Laws of Success, Charles I. Prosper. ISBN 978-0-943845-63-0

The Prophet, Kahil Gibran. ISBN 978-0394404288

The Sayings of Luzemily, The 7-Year Old Sage, Luzemily Prosper ISBN 978-0-943845-19-7

Think and Grow Rich, Napoleon Hill. ISBN 0-87980-444-0 (www.mpowers.com)

Unstoppable, The Incredible Power of Faith in Action, Nick Vujicic. ISBN 978-0307730893

Webster's New World Dictionary, (Revised and Updated.) ISBN 978-07434-7070-4

Charles I. Prosper
The Consistency Success-Coach™

About The Author

Charles I. Prosper (*The Consistency Success-Coach*™) helps people to achieve all of their important goals through mastering consistency, which is the secret of all success.

In this book, you learn how to:

- **Strengthen** your personal commitment to succeed consistently

- **Create** an action plan to accelerate your immediate progress

- **Diminish** indecision to realize what you truly want

- **Overcome** procrastination to make your goals a reality

- **Restore** the life life-purpose dream you may may have postponed

Mr. Prosper trained in marriage and family therapy for two years at Northcentral University's graduate school in Prescott Arizona and holds a Masters Degree in Psychology. Receive his FREE Online Consistency Success-Course. Go to www.charlesiprosper.com right now. You may also contact him at prosper@ charlesiprosper.com if you are interested in having him give a "Consistency-Success Seminar" for your school, church, or business organization.

Here's How Have to a Long and Successful Life

AT LAST! THE 12 LAWS OF SUCCESS REVEALED

By Charles I. Prosper

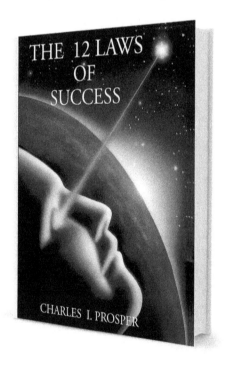

How to Get Rid of Stress and Worries for Good

207 MEDITATIONS FOR FINDING LASTING PEACE WITHIN YOURSELF

By Charles I. Prosper

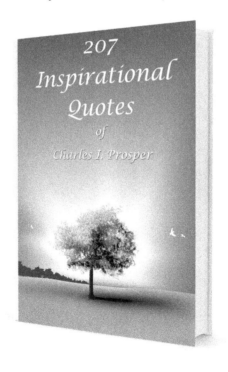

The World's First 7-Year Old Sage

Adults Who "Know It All" Are Not Invited to Read This Book

By Luzemily Prosper

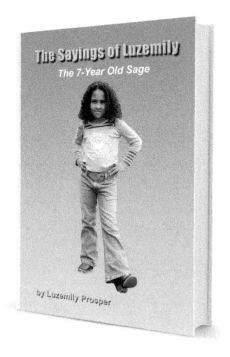

ANNOUNCING: A New System for Anyone Who Wants to Be Fit In the Next 12 Weeks!

YOU CAN BE FIT IN THE NEXT 90 DAYS

By Charles I. Prosper

BEFORE

amazon.com

90 DAYS

Why Some People Succeed at Whatever They Do

THOUSANDS HAVE THIS PRICELESS GIFT–BUT NEVER DISCOVER IT

By Charles I. Prosper

Why Consistency is the Key to All Success - and How to Be Consistent to Achieve Any Goal

Charles I. Prosper

amazon.com